Contents

Contents

Bright Ideas
Teacher
Handbooks
Reading

Acknowledgements

The publishers would like to thank the pupils and staff of the following schools for allowing us to photograph them at work for inclusion in this Handbook: Cherry Orchard County First School, Pershore; Whitmore Primary School, London; Anglesey Primary School, Birmingham; Brewster Primary School, Peterborough; Merrow Street Church of England First School, Guildford; Kemplah Country Primary School, Guisborough; Lakey Lane Primary School, Birmingham; Edgewick Infant and Junior School, Coventry; Royds Hall High School, Huddersfield; West End Middle School, Clecheaton.

The passage from *The Iron Man* on page 95 was reprinted by permission from Faber and Faber Limited.

The story 'The Little Storm' which appears on pages 87–89 also appears in *More Stories to Tell* edited by Eileen Colwell, published by Puffin Books. The Publishers have been unable to trace the original source.

Published by Scholastic Publications Ltd, Marlborough House, Holly Walk, Leamington Spa, Warwickshire CV32 4LS
© 1987 Scholastic Publications Ltd
Reprinted 1987

Contributors: Elizabeth Laycock, Liz Waterland, Barbara Dixon, Sue Pidgeon, Keith Topping, Elizabeth Wood, Irene Yates, Winsome McKay, Elaine Goddard-Tame.

Edited by Priscilla Chambers
Designed by Dave Cox
Sub-edited by Jackie Cunningham-Craig and Annette Heuser
Artwork by Jane Bottomley
Photographs by Dave Richardson, Keith Topping pages 47, 49, 52, 53, 75, 76, 77, 79, 80, 81 and 85

Printed in Great Britain by Ebenezer Baylis, Worcester.

ISBN 0 590 70691 8

Front and back covers: photograph by Martyn Chillmaid; Children's clothes courtesy of Mothercare; Cushions courtesy of Habitat.

Contents

TESTING AND KEEPING RECORDS 175 to 192

MULTICULTURAL APPROACHES TO READING 161 to 173

REPRODUCIBLE MATERIAL 194

INDEX 214

Introduction

Becoming literate ought, above all else, to be a joyful process. Spanning many years, the critical learnings of reading and writing – like learning to speak – engage each individual at a deep, person-making level and learning continues throughout life. The success of early learning strategies in those crucial years, and the pain or joy of that learning, determine the quality of literate activity throughout life.

If learning to speak were as painful and inefficient as learning to read and write proves to be for many children, the telephone would not dominate modern living as it does. Almost invariably, we enjoy talking because the early experiences were so good – so efficient in sustaining learning and so full of reward and joy. On what grounds do we assume that learning to read and write must be painful? The first priority of an efficient literacy program, regardless of methodology, is that it is a personally meaningful and joyful process.

We have come a long way in the last 15 years towards understanding and researching this most basic principle, and teachers of goodwill all over the world in classrooms and clinics have shown how it can be made real. Such a principle, taken with absolute seriousness, makes a mockery of all that is tedious and boring in rival methodologies of teaching basic skills – for, apart from pain, if there is anything which the human brain finds joyless, it is being bored. Our current willingness to accept this over-riding priority, reflected in these chapters, marks a turning away from 'reading schemes', as providing all the answers, towards a serious concern for learning – a turning towards the learner as a growing person; towards strategies and processes of learning rather than isolated skills; towards learning through doing from the earliest stages; and towards the use of a fascinating literature written by real authors who deeply desire to communicate with children rather than sham 'reading materials' concocted joylessly in the anterooms of editorial departments.

The history of ideas about teaching literacy makes a sad and chaotic picture of competing methodologies, denatured teaching materials, piously contested conflicts, dehumanising labels for failure, and rapidly rotating trends, bandwagons, and plain ballyhoo (to use a much-loved Kiwi expression). In contrast, the last few years have displayed a much more sane approach characterised by a focus on the conditions of efficient learning rather than on the dogmas of instructional method. Like the widely differing but equally effective methods of psychotherapy, teaching methods of great variety flower in classrooms, provided the central priorities of the learner are scrupulously maintained.

Learning to read and write can be, and ought to be, a natural process like so many of the other complex tasks which we learn developmentally. This implies learning by actually functioning in the skill and perceiving details and parts of the skill always in relationship to the whole which embraces it in purposeful action. Those learning to read and write need to process whole books, poems, and songs in a variety of ways as the central activity of 'instruction' *from the very beginning.* The term 'Whole language teaching' has been used increasingly to refer to the wide range of procedures which meet this criterion, but we would be wise to see this as a basic point of principle, drawing appropriately from all

the established 'methods' rather than as a new methodology. The authors of this book represent the richness and variety of procedures available to us in keeping learning whole.

We have no better models for effective language learning than those displayed in the joyful functionality of learning to speak and in the aggressive pre-school literacy of children from book-oriented homes. It is these developmental models which inform good literacy teaching today. This book of practical suggestions for teachers of reading is not intended to represent a systematic and coherent methodology – we have learned that success and joy are not achieved that way. The ideas presented here are the suggestions of talented practitioners who have themselves experienced the joys that may sustain young learners as they discover the satisfactions of print.

Reading materials and policy

Reading materials and policy

INTRODUCTION

Elizabeth Laycock has taught for many years in primary schools in Birmingham and London. After obtaining a Diploma in Professional Studies in Education (the Teaching and Reading) at Avery Hill College she went to work in Hackney as an advisory teacher with the Literacy Development Team. She is currently on secondment to the ILEA's Centre for Language in Primary Education. Although Elizabeth is an employee of ILEA the ideas presented in this article are her own and do not necessarily reflect those of the authority.

Although the focus of this book is on reading, language cannot really be separated into compartments. Talking, listening, reading and writing are inextricably bound together, and experiences in one mode affect learning in the others. Listening to stories and talking about them is as much a part of reading as decoding the print on the page. Equally, the experiences and expectations children have of reading, feed into their talking and writing.

Traditionally teachers have tended not only to separate language into conveniently teachable segments, but also to divide reading into teachable bits and pieces. The skills of reading – initial letters, consonant blending, vowel digraphs, word attack skills etc – have been painstakingly taught one step at a time, and usually out of context. But these attempts to simplify reading for teaching purposes have, in fact, made it harder for children to learn. Of course, many did learn to read, but probably in spite of such teaching rather than because of it. No child learns to talk because she is taught the separate skills in the correct sequence! Infants learn to talk because they need to communicate and are helped to do so by supportive adults; they learn because they are surrounded by whole language and want to join in. They do not learn in adult-prescribed sequences, but through taking risks, getting it wrong, refining, and trying again, by being in control themselves.

Increasingly, teachers are becoming convinced that the best way to teach reading is to start by showing children what is in it for them. By reading aloud to them and sharing books with them children will learn to regard reading as an enjoyable experience.

The way children learn to read is by reading and not by *doing* reading exercises. Furthermore, as Margaret Meek states in *Learning to Read* 'what the beginning reader reads makes all the difference to his view of reading'. Sometimes children get the impression that learning to read is about jumping over various hurdles in a race to get to the end before the others in the class. When 'what is read' is not important and is tedious and irrelevant, the young reader does not expect to become involved in a book or to derive pleasure from the experience of reading it.

These views will be reflected in the following discussion on how to establish a school policy, and on the selection of materials to create a stimulating reading environment. The suggestions made will be informed by the following concerns:

- that teachers should be less concerned with 'teaching' reading skills, and more concerned with enabling children to learn
- that children should see reading as a relevant and worthwhile activity, and not as a race to be finished as quickly as possible
- that reading should be enjoyable and contribute to personal development as well as be functional
- that children not only *can* but *do* read, and go on doing so into their adult lives
- that it is the teacher's responsibility to provide exciting books that children will want to read.

Establishing a school policy

All schools need to have thought about their approach to language teaching. It is clearly best if colleagues can agree to work in similar ways so that real continuity can be achieved between individual classrooms. A school 'language policy' or 'reading policy'

cannot be imposed without discussion. An agreed approach is more likely to become operative and to be effective if all the staff have been involved in the discussion and the decision making. Nor can such a policy be put together hurriedly: it takes time to assimilate ideas and to discuss the pros and cons openly. To allow time for discussion and to reach some agreement may mean that a policy will develop slowly over a period of months, or even a year or two. Such a time-span also allows the school to plan the resourcing of the policy, setting aside money to buy books and equipment.

The formulation of the policy has certain pre-requisites:

- an appreciation of what the theorists suggest is involved in learning to read
- recognition of the knowledge about language (or languages) that the children bring to school
- familiarity with children's books
- a willingness on the part of teachers to observe children and to spend time talking to them, and a willingness to keep careful records of what each child can do.

Where to start

The policy for the school should be informed by knowledge and understanding of the theory behind the practice: teachers must set alongside their own observations, the evidence gathered, over the last 15 or so years, by the researchers who have examined how children learn (see page 12 for list of suggested books).

The first phase of establishing a school language policy is to invest in some of the books and start reading! This is assuming of course that there are one or two interested teachers – perhaps the language post-holders? a curriculum co-ordinator? a deputy head? head of infants?

The second is to gather together all interested staff and talk about the ideas and theories presented in the books. It is important to allow space for people to express their doubts and fears. It is helpful if discussions can be minuted, and written up later to provide a resumé for any members of staff who join the school after the initial discussions.

The third phase is to decide where to begin. Children's books are probably the best starting point. Look at the books in your school. Which books are most valued by teachers and children? Decide what percentage of the school's money is to be spent on real books (as opposed to textbooks, language materials, workbooks).

You will need to discuss:

- who is responsible for ordering books?
- are all staff involved in deciding what should be bought?
- are multiple copies of some titles available so that children can read together?
- are books bought unseen from catalogues or are they known to a teacher?
- what criteria are used for assessing books?

Selecting books

The staff will need to agree on criteria for selection. The following may be useful starting points. (See also notes on 'Assessing reading schemes.')

- Are the books of good quality? Consider the quality of the writing, the illustration, the design and layout.
- Is there a balance? Aim to get a variety of different types of fiction, folk and fairy stories, information books, biography, poetry, picture books (for all ages), and to get books at a variety of levels, some that are easy to read and some that are demanding.
- Is there a variety of format? Hardback and paperback, long and short, heavily illustrated and little or no illustration.
- Which books are unacceptable? Are there any which are racist or sexist? Do they present positive representations of people of all cultures and classes, of girls and women?

Information books

As much care needs to be exercised in the selection of information books as in the selection of all other books. In addition to the criteria applied to the selection of fiction or reading schemes, further questions need to be considered:

- Is the information accurate? Many books (especially science, technology, geography) will be out of date and need to be replaced by more recent titles.
- Is the information given likely to extend the reader's knowledge or merely state what he already knows. In how much depth and detail is the subject covered?

- Is the text so 'simplified' for children that information is misleading or distorted? Often a book written for adults will more readily meet the needs of a child who is particularly interested and wants to find out about a subject.
- How accessible is the information? Is there a good index and a contents list?
- Are there page headings so that a child can locate information easily without having to read the whole book?
- Is a distinction made between fact and opinion?
- Do any illustrations/diagrams clarify and extend the text?

Organising books

Discussion will be needed about how the school's books are to be distributed and organised. If there is a teacher responsible for the library he will need to find out how the children, as well as colleagues, feel the library should be organised. Decisions will need to be made about how books are to be classified and categorised. Can a system be devised that all the children can understand and which helps them to locate what they want? Discuss how the books are to be

displayed. What sort of shelving is needed? Can small children see and reach the books? Can space be made to display a good number of books with their covers showing? Decide how loans are to be recorded. Investigate whether there are sources where collections of books (eg on particular themes or topics) can be borrowed. Your local education authority might have central resources. Alternatively try the local public library; the children's librarian is almost certain to be interested in your children's reading and willing to help.

Some schools make the school library the centre for books, and they are borrowed either by individuals, or in class collections which are regularly changed. Other schools allocate most of the fiction and poetry to classes and make the library the focus for information books and other audio-visual resources, from which classes select collections of books relevant to a particular topic or centre of interest as and when they are needed.

Each school needs to develop a system of organising the books which meets its own particular needs, and fits in with the way in which individual teachers work.

Wall displays of the children's favourite books make the classroom attractive and help to promote reading.

The arrival of new books

When new books arrive in school the whole community should have the chance to see them, to browse, and to choose some favourites. In this way everyone gets to know what is available and perhaps to discover new titles as well as re-discover forgotten favourites.

- Can new books be displayed in the staff room for a week or so, so that teachers can read some of them, discuss them and share their responses?
- How can new arrivals be introduced to the children? Could there be regular book assemblies? Special displays of new books in the library and classrooms? An author or illustrator featured for a few weeks, so that children become familiar with a particular range of books? You might even be able to invite the author or illustrator in to meet the children.
- Do parents get a chance to see new books, perhaps at a parents' meeting or an open day? Could they have access to the library?

New books should be displayed where all the school can examine them.

Classroom collections and book corners

Organising the space

The book corner should be planned and set out so that it looks inviting: books jumbled, spine out, on shelves, do not look very

exciting, and it is hard to make choices if books are categorised in ways you do not understand.

Involve the children in deciding how the books should be classified and displayed in their room. Such discussion will often draw their attention to books they

6

may not have noticed before, as well as help them to learn their way around what is available. Let them make collective decisions about what the categories should be and how the books should be displayed. You may need to experiment with the layout and classification in order to find out what works best.

Factors which may need to be considered might include:

- Shelving and storage. Do you need to replace old-fashioned shelves with hanging racks or storage-boxes?
- How can enlarged texts (both commercial big books and school made) be stored and/or displayed? Is an easel available to put these books on to read them?
- Could you feature a particular author or subject in a special display? Let children be responsible for these and change them regularly.
- Can you acquire a carpet, comfortable chairs, cushions, a low table?
- How can magazines, comics, newspapers be displayed/stored?
- Is there a place for the children's own published writing? Can this be given importance?
- Is there a range of books at different levels, bearing in mind that there is likely to be a spread of over five years in reading ability in any one class?
- Can a listening corner be set up with a selection of taped stories, a cassette player with headphones and copies of the stories on the tapes so that children can listen and follow the text?

Set up a listening corner so that children can listen to their favourite stories.

Assessing reading schemes

Reading schemes of one kind or another are still much in evidence. A great deal of money is spent on them despite the Bullock Report's comment (1975): 'We are certainly not advocating that the school should necessarily use one, and we welcome the enterprise of those schools which have successfully planned the teaching of reading without the use of a graded series.' (7.25) Some are very old and well established, others are very new. Teachers should read all publishers' blurb about reading schemes with a healthy scepticism, and formulate their own questions about reading scheme books that are already in the school as well as those belonging to new schemes being considered. As with any books, do not buy on the basis of catalogue descriptions without looking at them first. A list of exhibitions is available from the Educational Publishers Council. Look together with colleagues and discuss your responses. Questions that should be posed about reading schemes might include:

- Do the books look exciting and inviting, or do they all look the same? Do they have a boringly uniform format, cover picture, illustrative style? Are the books written by authors and illustrators, or are they written to a publisher's formula (with no writers being credited)? Do individual books have titles (other than 'Green Book 3' etc?) Would a child *choose* to read them? Would a child want to re-read any individual title again and again (as indeed they *do* with *Not Now Bernard* (McKee), or *Spot* (Eric Hill)?
- Read the books yourself. When you read them aloud does the language 'flow'? Does it sound like real language? Is the text cohesive? Does it 'hang together' or does it sound like random statements? Does each book have a proper story or topic of interest to a child? One way to test books is to try reading it starting from the back, or to read a few sentences in random order. If it doesn't sound any different it's not a real book!

Testing the books

Try some of the reading scheme books out on a few children. What do they think of them? What do they like or dislike? What comments do they make on the characters, the stories etc? Read one to an inexperienced/beginning reader, and get her to read it back to you. Can she retell the story? Compare this response with the same child's response to a real book such as *A Dark, Dark Tale* or *The Very Hungry Caterpillar*.

Accompanying materials

With any reading scheme you must also look at the supplementary materials, workbooks etc. What are they aiming to do? Will they help the child to read? What messages will they give to the child about reading, and what will she learn from them?

Read the teachers' handbook. What is the theoretical basis the compilers of the scheme are using? Do you agree with this? Are the children supposed to read every book? What activities are suggested as being essential/helpful for children?

The handbook should reveal a great deal about the rationale behind the scheme. Many of the newer ones appear to plan every lesson and step for the teacher, and leave no room for individuality either in teachers or children.

Finally, do these books really offer the things that children need to help them to learn to read, or will they help children learn that reading is a boring, meaningless activity that has to be tolerated in school, and that what matters is 'getting through' all these books as quickly as possible in order to please the teacher.

Using what you have

When you have really looked at what is in the various schemes the school has, and you have decided on those which are enjoyable and valuable, these can be incorporated into the library or classroom collections of books. You can combine the best of what you already have with new arrivals. Remember that before you abandon your schemes you must have something to put in their place.

Banding and colour coding

Many schools have adopted a system for putting all books (books from schemes and real books) into levels of difficulty. Most of these systems are based on Cliff Moon's *Individualised Reading*. Lists of books, divided into the appropriate stages (0–13), are published regularly by the Centre for the Teaching of Reading at Reading University. Cliff Moon explains at some length, the basis for these levels, in *A Question of Reading* (Moon and Raban).

The books are often colour coded in these levels and each child is given a free choice of books within that colour band. The rationale behind the coding is that children will not be required to follow the same rigid succession of books as everyone else in the class, thus making each child's reading experience unique.

Whether such a system is helpful to the individual child, may depend on how rigidly the levels are adhered to. Do you say to the child who has chosen a book two levels above the one you think is appropriate, 'No, you can't read that – it's too hard for you', or do you help her to read it, if she really wants to? In some classes 'individualised reading' differs very little from a reading scheme, because the children are required to read every book available at one level before being allowed on to the next.

The children are usually just as aware of the progression, and enter into the race as readily under a banding system as they do with a reading scheme. The aim is usually to get the next level or colour as quickly as possible, rather than linger over loved books at a lower level, or even go back to a favourite book at a much earlier level.

Readability

There are many scientific tests of readability (eg Fry's readability formula, Forcast readability formula, Spache readability formula) which can be applied to texts to determine their level of difficulty, or give them a 'reading age'. Most of them take several samples of 100–150 words from a text or book, apply the formula to the sentence length and/or the number of syllables in a word, average out the score on the samples, and arrive at a reading level. But, as Moira McKenzie points out in *Reading Matters* (McKenzie and Warlow), 'The problems of grading books are, of course, enormous. There are no standardised formulae that will quantify the comparative difficulty of, say, Eric Carle's *The Very Hungry Caterpillar* (only 18 sentences long, an interest level of four to six years, a lot of repetition, lavish illustrations and a text whose 'readability level' is ten) and Alan Garner's *The Owl Service* (173 pages long, no illustrations, a very obscure theme, but also a measured 'readability level' of less than ten)'. She goes on to point out that 'A completely effective

grading system would have to consider not just vocabulary and sentence structure but overall length, familiarity with text, narrative structure, illustrations and layout. . . .'

There are so many factors to be taken into account that it would be impossible to devise a test that could match every child with an appropriate book. A better practice would be to leave the matching of child to book to the classroom teacher who has a real knowledge of the books available and a real knowledge of the children in her class, including their interests, previous reading experiences, and an understanding of the sorts of stories each child will respond to.

Reading in the classroom

Each school will need to establish an agreement on the value of certain classroom activities. Examine what are the real reasons for the reading and writing that the children do. Do the children have the opportunity to collaborate and share their responses and knowledge? If the content of the curriculum is of interest to the children and they are invited to investigate, seek information and

record their responses and findings, a lot of reading, writing, talking and collaborating will be going on.

Consider the central importance of reading and ask yourself whether it has enough time in your busy curriculum. Should you make more time for reading? If so, you will probably find that some other things will have to go, and serious consideration needs to be given to the relative values of the different activities the children are being asked to undertake.

Reading aloud

Reading aloud to the children is perhaps the most important activity that there should be time set aside for. At the very early stages this sharing of books is the foundation of the child's understanding of what books and stories are about. If the experience and the stories are enjoyable and rewarding, the child's motivation to read will be all the stronger. Margaret Meek (*Learning to Read*) says, 'In the child's first few days of school the teacher will both read stories and tell them. The class comes together to listen, and there is a kind of communal spellbinding that holds them for as long as the story lasts, a shared experience that the children remember long after every one has learned to read for himself. Reading is a social as well as an individual activity in the early days, and right from the start a good teacher

Children of all ages enjoy hearing stories read aloud.

will encourage every child to see himself as a reader among readers. . . .'

Reading aloud should go on, even when the children are able to read independently. Teachers don't necessarily need to be the ones doing the reading. Invite parents and other adults to help.

In reading aloud sessions children can be introduced to books they could not tackle alone, and new vistas of what they can one day expect to read, can be opened up. Even lively adolescents can be caught up in the spell of a story that is read aloud. For those

who are the least independent the hearing of stories goes on being a powerful reminder of the pleasures to be found in books. Too often, the least able readers are the ones who encounter only the bits and pieces of language, and who are deprived of the satisfaction that is gained from encounters with whole stories – unless someone goes on reading aloud to them.

Personal reading

Children ought to be allowed the time and opportunity during the week for a variety of different kinds of reading.

They will need:

- time for browsing quietly amongst the books
- time to read alone for long periods of time
- time for shared reading aloud, in a group or with the whole class (see Chapter 3 on The shared reading approach)
- time to read in pairs or groups
- time to listen to taped stories
- time to 'read to learn', finding information for real purposes within real contexts
- time for occasional reading aloud to you, to each other or to a larger group.

Talking about books

Is there time for the children to talk about books?

- in groups of children, with or without the teacher?
- in a one-to-one situation with the teacher?
- with the whole class?

Talking about books will help children to relate experiences they read about to their own lives.

The children need to be helped to draw parallels between their current reading and other reading, between the experiences in the book and their own experiences. This will give them the chance to respond to the experiences of the book and to evaluate, and to talk about their own likes and dislikes so that they can learn about different responses in other people.

Writing related to books

- Can children sometimes record their responses, perhaps as reviews, so that others might be introduced to a particularly rewarding book?
- Is there a chance to write their own stories, coming from or related to books they have read?
- Could they write to favourite authors or illustrators and share their enjoyment or criticisms with the book's creators.
- Is there time to write their own original stories, poems, biographies, accounts etc for publication within the school and to add to the school's reading materials?

This school has found a unique way of displaying books written by children.

Recording progress

Part of the school's commitment to its reading policy must be a willingness to record what children have achieved and what they have read: any policy must aim for continuity. The recording becomes all the more important if reading schemes are abandoned or merged.

Observing and recording children's reading is even more important when reading schemes are not used.

Teachers will need to observe their children carefully and note their behaviour with books, their comments and responses, as well as the actual titles they have read, (other chapters in this book look in detail at ways of 'assessing what you hear').

Teachers need to be aware of how a child reads in different situations, how she responds to different sorts of books, whether she can use books as a tool for learning, whether there are difficulties which another teacher would need to be aware of.

There should also be some record of the books that have been read aloud to a particular group of children, so that over a period of years, a balance can be achieved between the different types: realistic fiction, fantasy, science fiction, humour, classics, biography, poetry, myth and legend, fairy story, picture books, information books etc.

11

Parents

Consideration of how to involve the parents as partners in the task of helping children to become literate should be part of the discussion amongst colleagues about their aims and policy.

Parents have, after all, supported their children's learning for five years before school began, and they should not be excluded from playing their part when formal teaching begins. (See chapters by Liz Waterland and Sue Pidgeon in this book.)

Schools will have different ways of keeping in touch with parents. However it is done, it is important to explain the way in which the school is working, to explain how they can share in this and to answer their questions and queries.

It is probable that the way reading is now taught is different from the way most parents were taught. It is important to explain why and how it is different. The school should have clear aims and be prepared to justify these and demonstrate the children's progress. Parents will not be able to play a part, and will become anxious if they do not know what is going on.

School and home should collaborate as each contributes to the child's reading development. Conflicting messages will confuse and distress a small child and hamper her progress (see chapter on Involving parents).

Resources

Learning to Read Margaret Meek, Bodley Head (1982)

The Foundation of Literacy Don Holdaway, Scholastic (1979)

Understanding Reading (3rd edition) Frank Smith, Holt, Reinhardt and Winston (1978)

Essays into Literacy Frank Smith, Cambridge University Press (1984)

Awakening to Literacy H Goelman, A Oberg, F Smith, Heinemann (1984)

Young Fluent Readers Margaret Clark, Heinemann (1976)

Read With Me : An Apprenticeship Approach to Reading Liz Waterland, Thimble Press (1985)

Learning to Read with Picture Books (3rd Edition) Jill Bennett, Thimble Press (1985)

Practical Ways to Teach Reading Cliff Moon (Ed), Ward Lock Educational (1985)

A Framework for Reading Somerfield, Torbe and Ward, Heinemann (1983)

What's Whole in Whole Language Ken Goodman, Scholastic (1985)

Language Jeff Hynds (Ed), Avery Hill Reading Centre, Bexley Road, London SE9 2PQ

Children Reading to Their Teachers National Association for Teachers of English (1985)

Children's Minds Margaret Donaldson Fontana/Collins (1978)

Books for Keeps published by School Bookshop Association, 1 Effingham Road, Lee, London SE12. Six times a year.

Children's Books for a Multicultural Society 0–7 and *Children's Books for a Multicultural Society, 8–12* Compiled by Judith Elkin, (Ed) Pat Triggs, School Bookshop Association, 1 Effingham Road, Lee, London SE12

The Good Book Guide to Children's Books Yearly, Published by Penguin.

Ways of Knowing (Information Books) Peggy Heeks, Signal (Thimble Press)

The Cool Web – The Pattern of Children's Reading Margaret Meek, Aidan Warlow and Griselda Barton, Bodley Head (1978)

Picture Books to Read Aloud Tried and Tested Group, Centre for Language in Primary Education ILEA

The Read Aloud Handbook Jim Trelease, Penguin

The apprenticeship approach

The apprenticeship approach

INTRODUCTION

Liz Waterland has taught for many years in primary schools in London and Peterborough and is at present deputy head at Brewster Avenue Infants School. Her own experience with teaching reading led her to write *Read, with me: An Apprenticeship Approach to Reading* published by Thimble Press. She now combines being a full time classroom teacher with giving talks to teachers and parents and writing articles on the apprenticeship approach to reading.

little ghost

People learn things best while doing them. Adults learn to drive while driving; children learn to speak while speaking.

Reading can be developed in just the same way. Traditionally children have been taught the various skills of reading individually on the assumption that they would then be able to put them together and become readers. Teaching reading in this way is rather like giving the child a jigsaw puzzle to do without providing the picture on the box. Think how hard that would make it! The skills of reading can only be meaningful if they arise out of the child's experience of being a reader; in order to learn to refine the tasks involved in reading, children must, paradoxically, be readers.

The child must also feel that reading is a richly rewarding experience, not just on the intellectual or competitive level but on the emotional and spiritual level. Therefore the books used must entice him to continue reading; they must be the best available – providing the child with a real reading experience.

Every child, however young, inexperienced or underprivileged needs to be given the chance to be a real reader in a real reading environment.

What is a 'real reader'? A toddler who sits transfixed by the pictures of cars or ducks in a board book, a child who spends so long in the library choosing a book that his mother gets cross and picks one for him, a little girl who sits so engrossed in her storybook that she doesn't hear the teacher say it is playtime – those are real readers.

This chapter will describe how you can create an environment in your school in which each child is an apprentice in reading, learning in the natural progression from experience to needed skills. It is hoped

Children learn to read by reading.

that the examples given will provide you with an understanding of the apprenticeship process and how it can be developed and adapted for your own use, no matter what stage of development your children are at.

Creating the environment

Objectives

The atmosphere of the school will strongly affect a child's desire and motivation to read. To help the child become an apprentice reader an atmosphere as much

like that of a good, loving home where books and reading are given a high priority should be created. This is important for all children, but especially for those who do not have such homes.

Level of development

At this stage it is your level of development and that of your colleagues and parents which you will be concerned with.

Ideally, the whole staff and the head will feel that it is time to change the school reading policy. They will have discussed and planned it together and will work as a team to make the changes needed. This is not always the case however. It might be that one or two enthusiastic teachers will be asked to run a pilot scheme for, say, a year, after which other classes will also undertake the change or, in the worst case one teacher or head will face hostility or indifference from the rest of the staff.

Try to make your book corner look like a 'good' home.

Whatever the situation, creating the right conditions depends on a knowledge of the basic rationale for apprenticeship approaches – without it, do not start.

The realness of a child's reading has nothing to do with competence in decoding but has to do with the love, involvement and pleasure that the child brings to books. It is a fragile relationship, especially at its beginning and can easily be shattered by insensitivity. It is important that teachers are careful they don't hinder its development or prevent it from even developing at all.

Think about what a 'good' home would look like. It would have books everywhere, in every room; not only on shelves but also on the floors and the chairs. It has comfortable places for children, cushions and mats on the floor, soft chairs to sit in. It would have loving adults to read to and with the child, explaining, helping, pointing things out, just when the child showed need. Best of all, it would have the child's own books of all sorts: old, new, big, small, easy, hard, silly and educational, and the child could choose when and what to read.

But how can you create such conditions at school? 'It sounds wonderful,' you say, 'just how my own daughter learned about reading, but with 30 children, a square box of a room and not much money how do I go about it?'

Teach yourself

The first move is to ensure that you and your colleagues, understand what you are going to do and why. You will need to read and think about what real readers do and how they develop. The Resources list at the end of the chapter (see page 33) will help you to get started. It is better to postpone your 'change over' for another term or so, than to start in a rush of ill-informed enthusiasm and then realise that you cannot really answer when a parent says, 'Why aren't the books coded anymore?'

Involving parents

The next task is to inform the parents what you will be doing and why. Some parents will naturally be concerned that you are abandoning reading schemes and workbooks. For most of them that will be their experience of learning to read and they will want to know why the apprenticeship approach is better. A useful strategy to take is to remind parents how their children have already learned to speak, eat, walk etc by working in partnership with adults. Explain that the school now wants to teach children about reading in the same way.

Tell the parents as much as you can about your plans: what you are going to do in school; how parents can help at home; what books are best; what the children will do. The more you let them see that you believe in what you are doing, the more they will trust you.

Provide a booklet for parents to take home after the meetings and ensure that they know they are welcome to come back with individual questions. See also the chapter on Involving parents (pages 47–56).

Classroom organisation

Whatever the age of your children, begin with examining your classroom (better still the whole school). Where are the books? Are they in a 'special place' labelled, coded, tidy? Begin by taking the stickers off (it is, after all, the child they are labelling) and by spreading the books around the room – into the home corner, the bricks corner – anywhere in the classroom.

Every classroom will need a reading corner. It will need a carpet, some cushions, even, if you're lucky, an old settee. You should aim to create a home environment within your work place. Parents may be helpful in providing soft furnishings, book boxes and shelves etc. The reading corner should be the heart of the classroom: it provides comfort, enticement, and fun. Above all, of course, it provides wonderful books.

The selection of books is dealt with in the next section; but it is important to remember that books are the purpose of learning to read, not just the tools of that learning. That means that books, print and literacy must have the highest priority in classroom organisation.

The way you display the books reflects your priorities. Display them facing outwards as far as room allows; put them in appealing places where they are always to hand as children work.

Home-made resources

When you are using the children's own writing as a reading resource you will need to give thought to their organisation. Writing develops hand in hand with reading and, as with reading, the resources and encouragement should surround the children constantly. Paper, pencils,

Your writing corner should be as enticing as your reading corner.

dictionaries, word banks and Sentence Maker equipment should always be available – as well as the free time to enable writing development.

Large empty detergent boxes are ideal holders for Sentence Maker folders, home-made books, and paper or word cards. Cut in half and covered in wrapping paper, they are strong and roomy.

Use them and shelving to create a writing corner – try to make it as enticing as your reading corner. A table, chairs and several sorts of writing tools (felt pens, thick and thin pencils) together with coloured media (pastels, pencils, crayons, chalks) and

This book box was made by a local youth training scheme.

various sizes and colours of papers will encourage experiments in writing. A stapler or hole punch and coloured wools will help the production of all kinds of books. Every child can be an author in such circumstances!

Treat the children's stories just as if they were real books. That is the way the child will see them. You will need a box or book rack in the reading corner where they can be displayed for children to read when they wish.

Taking your time

Children need time and support if they are truly to learn anything. Literacy is a quality of life, not a quantity of knowledge. Make sure to give yourself and your children ample time for reading. In a relaxing environment the children will be able to learn and to become readers. This is the essence of apprenticeship reading – the teacher's confidence and support for the emergent reader.

Choosing the books

Objectives

Because the sort of books offered to children are going to be crucial in shaping their perception of themselves as readers and their knowledge of what readers do, the choice of books is most important.

Choose books which have real quality, which have been written by a real author, not for teaching reading, but for the pleasure of writing a story for children. They should be written in natural whole

language with complete grammar and punctuation.

Take care to choose books which will appeal to the age of the child involved. With the apprenticeship approach there is no need to worry about vocabulary control, type face or numbers of words per page as you will be helping the child to read. Instead concentrate on whether the topic of the book and the illustrations will appeal to the child (See chapter on Assessing books, page 59 for essential points to look out for).

You will need to make sure that you, as a teacher of literacy, are informed and aware of the vast variety of children's literature so that you can make wise choices. This will enable you to choose books with souls: books written by authors who had something to say and which are emotionally involving. Beware of the plastic shrink wrapped books coming from the latest reading schemes. Most of these have no souls; no writer (or reader) ever loved the people in them, or really cared what happened to them.

Teach yourself about books

Choose your books by becoming involved in children's literature. Enlist the help of your school's librarian. Study publications such as *Books for Keeps*, *The Good Book Guide to Children's Books*, *Learning to Read with Picture Books*, *Reaching Out*, *Picture Books for Young People 9 to 13* and reviews in magazines such as *Child Education* or *Junior Education*. Best of all haunt your local bookshop, browse and sample until you feel you know what is on offer for your children.

Stocking up

If you have, as most schools do, a vast stock of reading schemes you will be most reluctant to 'waste' this expensive resource. Using the criteria mentioned above examine the books. If you feel that any of them measure up and if *you* like to read them then add them to your bookshelves. You will soon know if they stand up to comparison with other books by the use the children make of them!

Divert your new reading scheme money to real books. It is possible to provide your children with a stock of real literature without spending more money than you would for a new glossy reading scheme and you will have far more real value out of it. Several publishers produce collections of real books which enable you to buy at a discount. Use your school library allocation to the full. Start a bookshop or a book club and plough the profit back into buying books for the school. Ask friends to donate grown-out-of books. Haunt book sales; even jumble sales can be a source of extra books.

Level of development

Throughout the school.

Classroom organisation

When you have chosen the books you will need to put them where the children are: into the classrooms, the home corner, the brick corner or the writing area.

Organise your books only by the children's interest and the teacher's preference.

There is no need to colour code or arrange them by difficulty because if the children are being supported by an adult it does not matter whether they can read the books they choose independently, or indeed, whether they can read at all. It is just as important for a child to have a 'hard' book read to her as for her to read herself. How else will she learn what readers do and how literature works?

Children need to be given 'real books' if they are to learn to regard reading as an enjoyable activity.

Providing a role model for the child

Objectives

To enable your children to learn and benefit from the real reading environment, you should provide the opportunities for them to experience the full range of reading behaviours and to practise them for themselves. There are four behaviours which should be provided for, whatever the age or aptitude of the child:

- Listening to and watching fluent reading behaviour.
- Sharing a book with a more fluent reader; discussing written language; choosing and being critical of books.
- Initiating reading independently.
- Being an author.

The first of these will be dealt with in this section.

Level of development

Children of all ages benefit from having books read to them. It is particularly important however for beginning readers that they are presented with an example of what a reader does.

Classroom organisation

Class experience

The traditional 'story time' where the teacher reads a story to the class is an excellent way of demonstrating fluent reading behaviour. Make sure the children can see you following the print and that you have chosen a book that has real emotional quality. 'Big books', either published or homemade, are ideal for class story times (see the chapter on the Shared Reading approach for more details on how to use big books). Read the book early in the day; re-read it and let the children join in. Leave it around to stimulate further language work during the day. Provide the children with conventionally sized versions to take home or read to friends. In this way they can imitate the complete reading behaviour that you have been demonstrating.

Creating a weekly serial will help to show beginning readers the connection between speech and writing.

The weekly serial

A rewarding variation is for the class to write their own weekly serial. The children dictate a page a day and you write to their dictation on a large (A2) sheet with clear print (this speech into writing experience is very valuable, especially for beginners). The day's sheet can then be rewritten on smaller sheets (A4) and photocopied so that each child has a complete version of the story to take home and read. The big book can remain at school to be re-read whenever the children like. Older children might like to sustain such a story over several days.

Individual experience

Whole class experiences are not sufficient to provide the fluent reading model that children will need before they can begin to read on their own. For beginning readers especially, their initial introduction to reading with the teacher must be experience of the teacher reading a storybook to them, individually. Choose a book together with the child and, making sure you are both sitting comfortably, read the story for the child.

Teachers know how to do this already for we have been telling parents to do it for years. By providing such experience in school not only will the child learn how to be a reader; you will also learn from the child what he already knows and understands and what his needs are. It is the quality of this time, not its quantity that is important. Two five minutes sessions a week are far more valuable than two minutes every day. Let the child listen and discuss the text, point out interesting language patterns, hear what stories are and how written language works. Without this model of what a reader does the child cannot make sense of the details we may try to teach him later. Children from favoured homes have received this experience already. You must offer it to all children. It is important to note that all the 'input' at this stage should be from you. Do not require the child to produce 'output'. Forcing a child to perform, before he is either able or willing to do so, may damage his confidence. Encourage, but do not force, the child's contribution.

Sharing books

Objectives

Through the process of reading stories to children you will find yourself automatically providing opportunities for the second behaviour which children should experience – sharing books.

Level of development

As the children gain experience of listening to and watching a real reader they will want to share in the reading process. This is where sharing books together comes in. It is important to note that the two behaviours

are developed alongside each other (for experience of listening and watching continues at the same time as sharing).

Classroom organisation

Through the 'process' of reading aloud to the child, he will begin to contribute, to behave like a reader himself. He may recite a story with you, or point out an aspect of print that interests him ('that letter's in my name'). He may point out words he knows or try and point to the words as you read. He may say 'I can read this bit' or 'I'll tell you what happens'. All these responses indicate a confident real reader, a sharer (at whatever level of competence) in the process of reading.

Do not forget the role that other fluent readers can play. Invite parent helpers into the classroom to read with children or instigate a peer-pairing programme where older or more mature readers in the class or school can read with the immature reader.

Classroom assistants can give children valuable extra reading experience.

Encourage the child's parents to read a book at home each evening chosen by the child from the selection in the classroom. Brothers and sisters and other relatives can also help.

Learning about print skills

Through listening, watching and sharing books with a fluent reader the children are receiving input at their own, and at more advanced levels, and are being helped to contribute as much as they are able. They are also learning the specific skills of reading in apprenticeship with the fluent reader. They learn about punctuation, phonics, graphic clues, syntax and meaning as and when they arise in context, in meaningful stories and language.

During this time you should be noting, and later recording, what strategies the child is using. Observe how far he is behaving in a reading manner, what he shows he knows about story and the written code. You will need to watch and listen carefully.

Independent reading

Objectives

Children should be given experience in being able to initiate behaviour for

themselves, without the catalyst of the adult. This takes two forms, behaving like a reader, and being a reader. Both are equally valued and children should be encouraged to experience both (hence the importance of allowing access to all levels of book to all children).

You should allow children to use books at any time, not just when 'work' is 'finished'. You will see them picking up books, looking at the pictures, reciting well known stories and looking for bits of print

Reading should not be something which is only done 'when your work is finished'.

they know. Try to observe for a while, see if you can note and later record, what the child does when behaving like a reader. This unsupported behaviour shows you what a child *really* understands; it is important to study it.

Level of development

Even the youngest children should be given the opportunities to initiate independent reading.

Classroom organisation

Try to provide a time two or three times a week when all the children have 'quiet reading time'. This experience of being united in reading is very valuable and gives time for every child to be quiet and book-involved. Five or ten minutes is enough for four-year-olds, half an hour for tens or elevens. Don't forget you, too, should have a book to read. You are a reader, aren't you? Of course, many children will not, at first, be 'reading the words'. They will, however, be behaving like readers and seeing themselves as able to interact with a book on their own. The older the children, the more opportunities for independent reading and writing that should be provided.

This quiet reading period leads naturally to offering the opportunity for children to initiate their own reading. As in the ideal home described earlier in the chapter, you should be helping your children to read what and when they wish: this means you will need to be even more aware of the provision you make for children to choose books; non-fiction will need to be incorporated in the choice. You will need to be sensitive to the child's need for support or independence, depending on the child's view of himself and the text. Your shared reading sessions may need to continue for years if a child is immature or has learning problems. The child may, conversely, decide to take over the reading process within weeks of starting school ('I'll read to you if you don't mind, it's more fun').

Progression

Children's first experience of independent reading usually comes from reading their own stories. From there they typically progress to recognition of familiar words in print. As their knowledge of print skills grows they may attempt to read, first with adult support and then independently, starting with familiar stories. Gradually they will gain the confidence to tackle new texts independently.

Using the child's own text

Objectives

Children learn to read through a desire to hear and read meaningful text. For them it is their own experience that matters most. It is because of this intense personal experience that being an author, making their own text to read, is so important.

Level of development

Any child can be an author. You may need to do the writing for them initially but this does not detract from the fact that they created it and are able to read it back – just as an adult author would.

Classroom organisation

Many of the writing activities carried out in the classroom will need only a slight change of focus to provide the child with the chance of being his own author. When a child dictates a caption to a painting make sure he has an opportunity to read it back perhaps to his parent, perhaps to the class. When he dictates a story to you, read it back to the class as you would a 'real book' at story time.

Breakthrough to Literacy materials are an excellent resource for encouraging children to write (see Resources list, page 33). By using Sentence Makers you give your children the chance to make meaningful reading material of their own, about their own friends and family. You give them knowledge of how the written code works and fits together and a sight vocabulary of words which they will find frequently in printed books. This last is especially valuable as a way of learning to read the carrier words which are the least easy to get from context.

To start with, work with the teacher's Sentence Maker can be done in class or group sessions three times a week. Once the

Sentence Makers are invaluable for encouraging children to do their own writing.

children are familiar with how it works, they should have their own Sentence Makers and should 'make a story' at least three times a week. Write these first 'stories' into blank books (about six pages is an ideal size) for the children. Then one of the reading sessions each week should involve the child reading his own book, to the teacher. As each book is finished it can be taken home for the child to read it to his parents.

Even very young children enjoy writing their own stories.

Using the writing corner

As the child's own writing becomes legible (to him) he can take over the recording process. Later still, he will no longer need to make his sentence but will only need to have help with writing those words that are unfamiliar to him. Whatever his stage of development, the stories he makes should be treated with equal respect as printed books are and used as a reading resource just as often as a printed book.

You will be surprised how complex children's own reading material will be, and how easily they can read it back.

Put the children's writing into the book corner for use alongside printed books. Many children love to read their books to the class in story time. Another fun idea is to have a 'swop' time when they choose a friend's book to read and so learn the pleasure of entering into another person's meaning.

Their own writing provides most children with their first experience of independent reading; it is the reading of the writing that makes it their own. By providing this experience you are ensuring truly literate children – those who are in charge of the written word.

Monitoring and recording progress

Objectives

It is very important to watch, monitor and record your children's growing understanding of the reading process. Only in this way can you do your job as a teacher and plan the experiences the child needs to gain further independence.

The object of monitoring is to see what a child can already do; to record his behaviour for future reference; and to plan for further experiences.

Level of development

Children at all levels will need to have their reading progress monitored.

Classroom organisation

To assess the child's knowledge of the written code you will need to watch carefully what she does when being read to, when sharing reading or when reading for herself. This is why reading sessions with the teacher should be longer than is conventionally needed. There must be time to discuss, watch and help the child. Ask yourself such questions as:

- Does she understand that the message is in the print?
- Does she know the left-right convention?
- Does he understand the meaning of the story?
- Does he use grammatical or context clues to help prediction?

Refer to *Read with Me* and *What did I Write?* (see Resources list, page 33) for an outline of the progression to look for in understanding print and writing.

Until you know what a child already understands, you will not know what else he needs to learn. This aspect of the teacher's job is one of the most important if the child is to develop through apprenticeship approaches.

Recording

Recording the child's progress will enable you to assess what skills the child has acquired and which ones he still needs work on. By recording your observations you will be able to confirm your knowledge of the child's progress and better define it. It is also, of course, essential for the child's next teacher, the parents, as well as for the child himself to be given some feedback. If you are running a pilot scheme, accurate records will help you to demonstrate the effectiveness of the approach.

But how do you record? The old style straight line tick list implies that knowledge is gained in an orderly progression and therefore is not very satisfactory. A pictorial representation such as a circle is a possible alternative. The records shown here are only examples but suggest the sort of things which need to be monitored. It is not the number of books or titles or phonics lists

which indicate what a child understands but what she actually does with the written word. This is what needs recording.

Follow-up

Your record sheet will indicate the gaps in the child's understanding and where further knowledge is necessary for him to gain full reading fluency. From this you can plan what you need to encourage the child to do next.

Take one skill at a time. If the child shows a new behaviour whilst reading with you, work on that newly acquired skill. For example if the child uses an initial phonic clue for the first time show her how to use it more consistently. Point out initial sounds and explain how they help to confirm a context triggered guess. When the child can consistently show understanding of this skill record it on your record sheet.

To use another example, you may feel the child needs to gain more confidence in using syntax as a word attack skill. When you read with her show how the grammatical sense of the text can help to confirm a guess. This could be done by encouraging play with changing present to past tense, or singular to plural, until the child adds this skill to her techniques for reading.

This is the heart of the teacher's job – to lead the child along until he gradually takes possession of the knowledge that will make him a reader.

Reading behaviour record

Child's name _____ date of birth _____

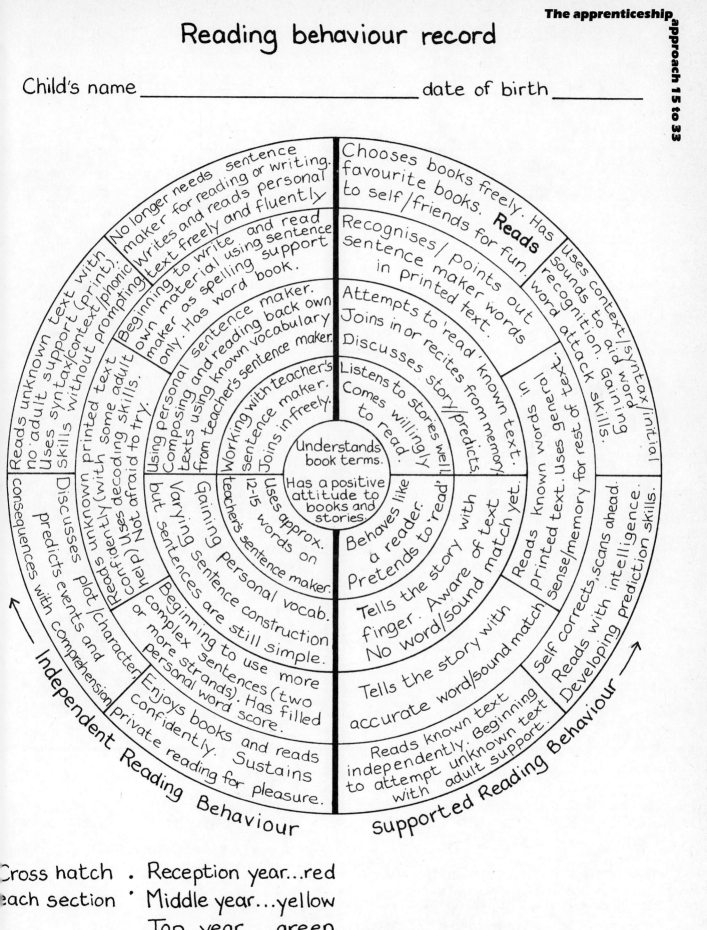

Reads

(Wheel diagram — sections from outer to inner ring)

Chooses books freely. Has favourite books. Reads for fun.

Recognises/points out sentence maker words in printed text.

Attempts to 'read' known text.

Joins in or recites from memory.

Discusses story/predicts.

Listens to stories well. Comes willingly to read.

Understands book terms. Has a positive attitude to books and stories.

Behaves like a reader. Pretends to 'read'.

Tells the story with finger. Aware of text. No word/sound match yet.

Tells the story with accurate word/sound match.

Reads known text independently. Beginning to attempt unknown text with adult support.

Reads known words in printed text. Uses general sense/memory for rest of text.

Self corrects, scans ahead. Reads with intelligence. Developing prediction skills.

Uses context/syntax/initial sounds to aid word recognition. Gaining word attack skills.

No longer needs sentence maker for reading or writing. Writes and reads personal text freely and fluently.

Beginning to write and read own material using sentence maker as spelling support only. Has word book.

Composing and reading back own personal sentence maker. Texts using known vocabulary from teacher's sentence maker.

Working with teacher's sentence maker. Joins in freely.

Uses approx. 12-15 words on teacher's sentence maker.

Uses personal vocab.

Gaining personal sentence construction — sentences are still simple.

Beginning to use more complex sentences (two or more strands). Has filled personal word score.

Enjoys books and reads confidently. Sustains private reading for pleasure.

Discusses plot/character, predicts events and consequences with comprehension.

Reads unknown printed text confidently (with some adult help). Uses decoding skills. Not afraid to try.

Reads unknown text with no adult support (print). Uses syntax/context/phonic skills without prompting.

Independent Reading Behaviour

Supported Reading Behaviour

Cross hatch each section

- Reception year...red
- Middle year...yellow
- Top year....green

© Brewster Avenue County Infants School, Peterborough

31

Written language development record

Child's name _____ date of birth _____

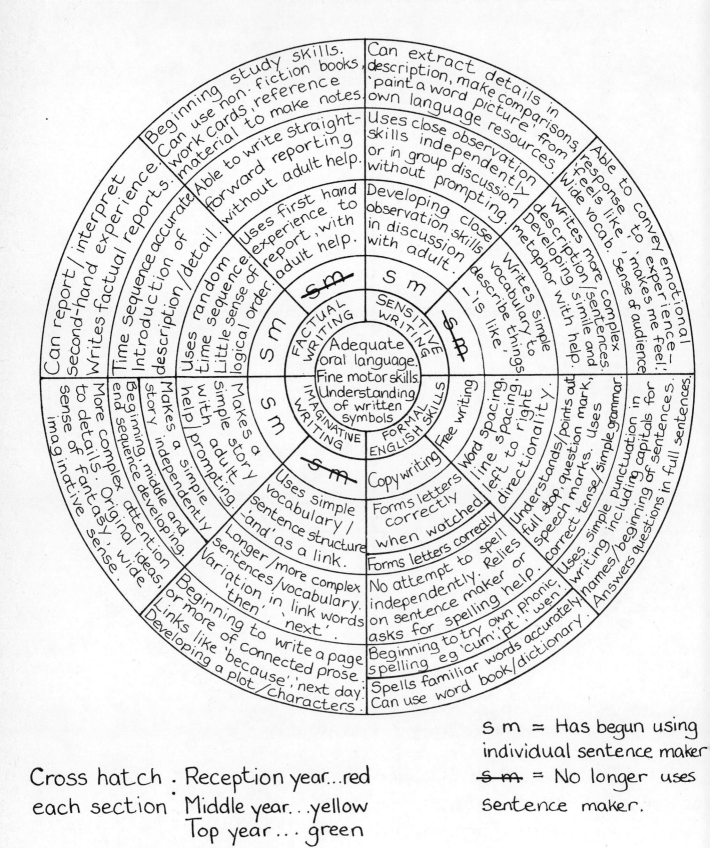

s m = Has begun using individual sentence maker

~~s m~~ = No longer uses sentence maker.

Cross hatch : Reception year...red
each section Middle year...yellow
              Top year... green

Resources

Learning to Read With Picture Books Jill Bennett, Thimble Press (1985)

What Did I Write? Marie Clay, Heinemann (1975)

The Foundations of Literacy Don Holdaway, Ashton-Scholastic (1979)

Recent Developments in Reading and their Implications Jeff Hynds (Ed), Avery Hill Reading Centre, Bexley Road, London SE9 2PQ (1984)

Breakthrough to Literacy Teachers Manual Mackay, Thompson and Schaub, Longman (1979)

Practical Ways to Teach Reading Cliff Moon, Ward Lock (1985)

Reading (2nd Edition) Frank Smith, Cambridge University Press (1985)

Reading Like a Writer Frank Smith, Centre for the Teaching of Reading, University of Reading (1985).

Read With Me: An Apprenticeship Approach to Reading Liz Waterland, Thimble Press (1985)

Books for Keeps published by the School Bookshop Association, 1 Effingham Road, Lee, London SE1Z 8NZ. Six times a year.

Books for your Children published by Anne and Barrie Wood, PO Box 507, Harborne, Birmingham B17 8PJ. Quarterly.

Child Education published by Scholastic. Monthly.

Junior Education published by Scholastic. Monthly.

The Good Book Guide to Children's Books published by Penguin. Yearly.

The Signal Selection of Children's Books published by Thimble Press. Yearly.

Learning to Read Margaret Meek, The Bodley Head (1982).

Practical Ways to Teaching Writing Bridie Raban (ed), Ward Lock (1985).

The shared reading approach

The shared reading approach

INTRODUCTION

Barbara Dixon trained as a mature student at the College of Ripon and York St John. She has taught in Essex, West Riding (Yorkshire) and in British Columbia, Canada. In 1980 she studied for an MA at Leeds University in the study of language development and beginning reading. She now teaches at North Riding College.

Becoming literate is an extension of the complex and lengthy process of language learning. When children learn to speak they pass through certain well-defined stages. Their speech gradually comes close to adult speech over a period of approximately three years. Even then, however, the process is by no means complete. They continue to refine their knowledge and adjust their speech accordingly throughout the primary years and beyond.

Studies of children who have learned to read early, without formal schooling or instruction, have shown that these children have had stories read to them, and have been allowed to explore storybooks for themselves, for anything between three and five years before they went to school. Other studies of early literacy show that such

children are encouraged to use writing materials and to take part in family activities when, for example, letters and notes are sent to others.

In homes where a lot of printed and written material is available, where parents share stories, songs, poems and nursery rhymes and children are encouraged to handle books, they gain an early understanding of the purpose of books. Gradually, they come to understand that, whilst the pictures are important and support the text, it is the *print* which represents the words and which renders the message permanent and unchanging.

By becoming familiar with books containing songs and stories, the child will be able to identify with the role of a reader as he tells himself the story. At first, he tells his own version, concentrating upon the meaning of the whole story and not just upon isolated fragments of text or words. In 'reading homes' this 'reading-like' behaviour is accepted and rewarded in an atmosphere which is not competitive and is rarely corrective. Self-confidence is developed because it is the child who has chosen the books on which to work. His learning is self-motivated and his reading eventually becomes more accurate through self-correction.

In such successful reading environments, the child is responsible for the pace of his own learning. Studies have shown that initially the child's language is usually extremely fluent and expressive. As he gains more experience and accuracy in recognising words and becomes more aware of the role print plays in reading, this reading-like behaviour will become more arhythmic, as Doake (1985) has pointed out. The child will try to match what he is saying with what he is seeing on the page and start to point to the words with voice and/or fingers.

Of course the adult has a vital part in this learning. She is responsible for motivation, by sharing the enjoyment of books with the child. As Leila Berg explains: 'Soon he will begin to "read" the story aloud himself, imitating and reproducing what the adult read that filled him with such delight when he heard it – just as he imitated and reproduced his parents' language earlier when he couldn't say separate words but only the tune. Now the magic of the word is extending even more.'

Shared reading is a term used to describe this 'apprenticeship' approach to reading. Through shared reading, a great deal of learning takes place. Firstly, when opening the book, turning the pages and perhaps pointing to the print as it is read, the adult is leading the child towards an understanding of the left-to-right and other directionality and conventions of English printed books.

Secondly, the child is being introduced to the language of books. Written language in continuous text differs considerably from everyday speech. Sentences tend to be longer and more complex and vocabulary is much more varied. Conversations, especially with children, tend to be about the 'here and now' and about things they can see, hear or touch. In reading, only the text itself provides the setting or context.

Children have to learn that words such as 'I', 'you' or 'here' do not refer to the person who is reading the story nor the setting within which it is read, but that they refer to imaginary persons in an imaginary setting. This ability to transport the reader, and listener, into a world of the imagination is perhaps one of the most potent features of story language. This is something which children only come to understand gradually through repeated exposure to stories. Learning the language of books extends children's powers of imagination and language immeasurably.

Through being read to children are introduced to the language of books.

As children move into solving the problems of matching the story they know to the marks on the page, the adult is again an essential provider of information. Margaret Clark in her study of young fluent readers emphasised the crucial role of the 'interested adult' in providing information on request about the child's self-imposed task. The significance of this is that it is the child who is asking for information *when he needs it*. In other words, the child has already developed the necessary understanding to enable him to use it.

Children who have had this kind of background arrive at school with an understanding of what to expect of books. They have the framework of thinking into which they can fit the kinds of information and experiences which school offers them. Some, of course, are reading already.

In contrast, many children come to school having had little or no experience with books and writing. They regard reading as a mysterious activity and have only the vaguest of expectations about books. These children are easily confused by the language of reading instruction. Terms such as 'word', 'letter', 'sound', 'sentence', 'beginning', and 'end', whether referring to speech sounds or written symbols, are meaningless and are, therefore ignored or forgotten.

Teachers of reception classes have always known instinctively that it is extensive pre-school experience with books and written language that is crucial to a child's ability to learn to read. Research carried out in many parts of the world now conclusively confirms this intuition. Can a parallel in the classroom be provided to this 'natural' development towards literacy?

It is possible to provide models of the activities, motivation for learning and opportunities for repetition of favourite stories on demand. It is possible to organise the classroom in such a way as to provide opportunities for children to work, at their own speed and at times they choose, on their favourite materials. Of course, the difference in the ratio of adults to children between the home and the classroom has to be taken into account, but this can be offset to some extent by involving children in the responsibility for their own learning and by enlisting the help of other adults (see Chapter on Involving parents, page 47).

A listening corner will enable children to listen to their favourite stories as often as they wish.

Reading to children

Objective

To encourage shared reading.

Level of development

Throughout the school.

Classroom organisation

In order to mimic a good 'reading home' the teacher should spend a large proportion of his time reading to the children. Storytime is far too important to be left to the last half-hour of each day. Two or three story sessions daily should be the minimum so that a wide variety of interesting material is introduced to the children from which they can select their favourites. Choose stories that contain repetitions of a formula of words which children can recognise, with enjoyable rhythms, rhymes and other patterns.

Pattern is very important in learning and particularly in language learning. Children make sense of the world by seeking patterns in their daily lives. Very young children use these patterns of events to bring meaning to the speech they hear around them, at bath times or feeding times, for example.

Some of the first patterns of words that children learn are those of the games played with babies. 'Peep-bo', 'Round and Round the Garden' and 'Pat-a-cake' or 'This little Piggy' link patterned language routines with tickling, patting or touching rituals. They are predictable and fun and the delighted infant demands repetition. Researchers of children's language development know that young children are fascinated with patterns of sounds and words. Many writers for children have in the past exploited this to great effect, for example, A A Milne and Lewis Carroll. Patterns of sound and words in songs, chants, rhymes and poetry introduce children to the language of books.

Repetition, rhyme and rhythm are particularly important. They provide predictability and support for the listener and beginning reader. Also, stories incorporating a refrain, such as *The Gingerbread Man* or *The Little Red Hen and the Grains of Wheat*, as well as more modern tales such as *The Very Hungry Caterpillar* or *Mr Magnolia* which incorporate sequences such as the days of the week or numbers one to ten. Bill Martin, an American researcher and writer reminds us: 'If a child doesn't have a sufficient repertoire of oral language

39

structures, the school's first job is to enter them into his ear in such enticing ways that he will reach out to claim them as his own.'

Songs, chants and poems should be a part of the daily classroom programme and well-loved ones should be written out and displayed for the children to read together.

Visibility

Another element of success in creating good readers at home is the fact that a child in a one-to-one relationship can see and follow the text whilst he shares a book. It is important to re-create this situation in school. The print should be clearly visible to all the children sharing the story and the teacher should point to it as she reads. The books should, therefore, be big enough for each child in the group or class to see the pictures and the print clearly.

Big books should be displayed on an easel so that children can go back to them throughout the day.

Frank Smith points out: 'It is important to read to children but even more important to read with them. Children get their first chance to solve many of the problems of reading when they and adults are reading the same text as the same time.'

The stories should be read with the children on more than one occasion and the children should be encouraged to join in and share the reading. It does not matter if they are all at different stages of understanding. Each child will take from the experience the information about the task and the knowledge about books that she is ready to absorb. Some children will be able to read along with the teacher, others to join in with the repetitions; some will just have begun to pay careful attention to the print and others just enjoy the stories and pictures. Enlarged books provide motivation and interest for them all.

Daily shared reading of enlarged books provides a model of the reading process and information about how books work. This comfortable, assisted reading within a group setting gives children an opportunity to acquire a sight vocabulary of common function words within a meaningful context – especially those words which, if presented in isolation, are so difficult to decode, for example, 'the', 'come', 'here' etc.

Shared reading is an enjoyable experience for the whole class, a stimulus for painting drama, retelling or writing or for further reading. Whole, meaningful stories such as *The Elephant and the Bad Baby* or *Brown Bear, Brown Bear* will bear repetition, examination, discussion and extension as opposed to the mistakenly over-simplified early readers, many of which have been denuded of all meaning and interest. In other words, enlarged books provide the nearest simulation to the bedtime story setting that it is possible to provide for a group of children in school.

'Big Books' belong from day one in the nursery or reception class. They have immediate visual impact; they use meaningful and memorable language; they stimulate children's interest and they are fun. A wide experience of stimulating and interesting materials should be provided over an extensive period before children are exposed to controlled reading programmes, and should be continued alongside such programmes throughout the primary years. The HMI report published in 1982 found that: 'Children were introduced too quickly to published reading schemes and there was too much concentration on the basic reading scheme.' (*HMSO 1982*)

Favourite stories for individual children in a class can be repeated in different ways. Firstly, the class can share favourites more than once. Secondly, by making use of volunteer readers, each child can have her own story re-read. Teacher aides, older pupils, parents, grandparents or other interested adults can be recruited and stationed in the book corner to read to children on request.

Listening to books

Another way is to make story tapes to be used in a 'listening centre'. Making the tapes is easy and the children are often delighted to hear the teacher's voice on the tape. Children soon learn to operate a cassette recorder correctly. Remember to take time on the tape to talk about the book – the cover, the author, the illustrations – and to help the child find the beginning of the story. Also, give the child time to look at the picture on each page. Use a signal to indicate when to turn the page. A junction box with headsets allows more than one child to listen at one time and encourages sharing.

More than one copy of the normal-sized version of storybooks allows children to share their listening and their learning. Shared 'reading like behaviour' is a potent way of learning to read.

To begin with, it is pleasurable, stress-free and non-competitive. Children read their favourite stories together. They will accept help and correction from one another with no loss of face as they assist one another to re-create the text. This is a very different situation to the old round-robin group reading which could be so embarrassing for the slower, less successful reader and so boring for the quicker ones. It is also, as a co-operative activity, very different to the individual reading to the teacher, which is really a test situation and one not always looked forward to by emerging readers.

Emergent reading

'Emergent reading' is a term coined by Don Holdaway who, with his team of teachers, pioneered Shared Reading in New Zealand.

Having more than one copy of a book allows children to share their listening and their learning.

In his book *The Foundations of Literacy* he documents their progress, their doubts and their successes and identifies different stages in the development of early reading. The central message of the book, and the central tenet of this approach, is that reading does emerge over time and through a series of successive approximations *given the same supportive environment that children enjoy when learning language in the home.*

The classroom must be 'print saturated' with a wide variety of attractive reading materials. Enjoyment of books, interest in all the purposes of writing and sharing the reading of motivating, meaningful stories form the core of the programme.

The teacher should immediately reward *meaningful* approximations to the text and minimise correction instead of insisting upon error-free performance from the beginning. Constant interruption for correction leads to loss of meaning and to monotonous 'word-calling'.

Competition between children, which is an in-built feature of every graded, coded reading scheme, ought to be discouraged. Children should be encouraged to concentrate on the purpose and enjoyment of reading.

Understanding meaning is more important than decoding. You can give necessary information about letter/sound relationships within the context of the story and where it is appropriate for the stage of understanding of individual children. This aspect arises naturally in their efforts at writing too.

Big Books are an ideal tool for teaching reading strategies. Shared reading activities such as group cloze procedure and group prediction teach children to be thoughtful, reflective readers. They also demonstrate to children that they already have skills and knowledge relevant to the task.

Children enjoy making and reading their own big books.

Point to the words as you read the story.

If only normal-sized versions of books for group story reading are used, not more than one or two children at the front of the group can see the pictures, let alone the print.

Group 'cloze techniques', where certain words in the text are obscured – for example, by a strip of card – can be introduced quite early into shared reading. The children are then invited to predict what the word could be. In this way they are required to search for a meaningful word, using the sense of the story and their own knowledge of how words are ordered in sentences. Sharing discussion with the group supports children in making predictions. In turn this develops confidence in using these strategies when reading alone. Group prediction can be introduced by simply stopping during the reading and inviting discussion about what could happen next. This again promotes the use of story context and requires children to monitor their reading (or listening) for meaning.

Using patterned and predictable texts which all the group can see clearly, provides opportunities for the children to examine the print more closely. The teacher can draw attention to similarities in the patterns of print and can teach about letter/sound

relationships. At an appropriate stage in their growing understanding of these relationships, children can be taught to use the letters of unknown (or temporarily covered) words to confirm or correct their predictions.

Group work of this kind is valuable teaching. It provides more support for the individual child and makes better use of teacher time than trying to hear each child read every day, which is a well-nigh impossible task. Vera Southgate found that: 'It is frequently unnecessary, rarely of sufficient duration to be effective and wasteful of the teacher's time.'

The Bullock report, wholeheartedly supported by Vera Southgate recommended: 'The best method of organising reading to be the one where the teacher varies the experience between individual, group and class situations according to the purpose in hand.' (*HMSO 1975*)

Of course, for diagnostic purposes, there is still a need to hear individual children read, but if the children are entrusted to get on with their reading-like-behaviour, the teacher has more time to spend with any one individual, perhaps using a tape-recorder to obtain examples of reading behaviour for analysis of strategies.

In science, in mathematical thinking, in social learning and oral language learning we acknowledge the value of co-operative activity. It is equally important in reading.

It is easy to overestimate what children know about reading, assuming for example that they all understand the purposes of literacy and are therefore motivated to learn. At the same time it is possible to underestimate their ability to be responsible for their own learning. Teachers need to provide a model and at the same time offer all the information children need about reading; but children should not be expected to give an error-free performance from the beginning.

Learning to read, like other developmental tasks, especially the acquisition of language, takes time. It may be encouraged, even accelerated, in a positive, supportive environment. It may be retarded by fear of failure. It cannot be hurried ahead of a child's understanding, nor is it easily accomplished by using materials which are over-simplified and denuded of meaning.

If you have multiple copies of book, some children will be able to follow along in their own copies as you read the big book.

Resources

Reading and Loving L Berg, Routledge and Kegan Paul (1977)

Young Fluent Readers M M Clark, Heinemann (1976)

A Language for Life D.E.S. HMSO (1982)

Education 5–9 D.E.S. HMSO (1982)

The Foundations of Literacy D Holdaway, Scholastic (1979)

Reading F Smith, Cambridge University Press (1978)

Extending Beginning Reading V Southgate et al, Heinemann (1981)

Reading like behaviour; Its role in learning to read D B Doake in *Observing the Language Learner*, A Jaggar, N T Smith-Burke, IRA/NCTE (1985)

Involving parents

Involving parents

INTRODUCTION

Sue Pidgeon has been teaching since 1970 in primary schools in the London area. For the past two years she has been one of two ILEA reading advisers. She is now a lecturer in primary education at Goldsmith's College.

It is not so long ago that parents were actively discouraged from coming into school. They were expected to deliver and collect their children from the playground gates. Those who dared to enter the building found the corridors were emblazoned with signs such as 'Please make an appointment before visiting the school' and 'Parents are requested to wait outside'. Teachers sometimes encouraged children to take their books home but it was felt that parents should leave the 'teaching' to those who knew how. Not surprisingly, many parents found this frustrating. They knew they had been important in their child's development up to that point, and felt disappointed that there were no opportunities to extend this involvement once the child had started school.

The scene in primary schools today is thankfully very different. The change in attitudes towards parental involvement has been one of the most significant steps forward in primary education in the last 15 years. The Plowden Report, in 1967, recognised the importance of good home/school relationships. This report and subsequent research has shown that parental involvement has a beneficial effect on a child's progress at school. Since then primary schools have been making very positive efforts to involve parents in their child's education. They are no longer the closed institutions they once were, but have parents' rooms and parents' associations; parents are encouraged to come in and work in the school alongside teachers. There is more feeling of co-operation and collaboration between home and school.

It is not only parents who are now involved in school activities. Other relatives, old age pensioners and other volunteers are asked to help out.

It has only been in the last five years or so that attention has turned towards parental involvement in children's reading. This is partly as a result of successful co-operation between home and school in other areas and partly as a result of changes in thinking about how children learn to read. Recent research into how children learn to read shows that literary experiences at home play an important role. Margaret Clark, Don Holdaway and Gordon Wells all found that children's pre-school experiences at home with books affected the ease with which they learnt to read. Similarly Jennie Ingham's study in Bradford showed that there was a definite likelihood that in homes where parents read a great deal the children would also.

The benefits

Schools that encourage parental participation in reading reap the benefits. It is such commonsense that you wonder why it took so long to realise it! The only way to get better at reading is by actually doing it, and children who are reading at home and at school are obviously reading more than those who read only at school. This has been confirmed by experimental projects such as the one carried out in Haringay, which compared children who read both at home and school with those who only read at school.

These results have encouraged more schools to become actively involved in developing home/school reading links. For example, some schools in Hackney, North London, set up PACT (Parents and Children and Teachers), a scheme whereby parents committed themselves to regularly hearing their child read and exchanged written comments about their child's reading with the teacher. (This is more fully described in *Parent, Teacher and Child*, and in the PACT booklet, see resource list on page 56).

Teachers are in a position now to positively encourage parental support at home for their children's reading, and to extend the post-Plowden ideals at home/school collaboration into the area of reading.

Young and old both gain from reading together.

Setting up your programme

Objectives

The long term aim of teaching reading should be that more children will read better, and see the pleasure and purpose in reading so that they will not only read at school, but choose to go on reading at home and when they have left school.

Involving parents not only gives children more opportunities to read. It also makes it clear that reading is something that is valued at home as well as at school. If you are going to encourage parental participation it is vital that you believe in and value the contribution parents can make. Parents are the most important influence on their children's lives; they are their children's natural teachers. Just as they were responsible for all their children's pre-school learning, they can continue to play a major part in furthering their children's development.

Parental involvement does not mean that teachers are shirking their role, nor does it mean that they are asking parent to 'teach' the mechanics of reading (the kind of rigid approach many parents remember from their own experiences of learning to read). Instead parents are being asked to work with teachers in order to put across to children the enjoyment and pleasure they can get from reading. By sharing books with their children, talking about books, reading to their children and hearing their children read, parents are helping their children's reading develop with enjoyment and understanding.

Level of development

Encouraging parental support for their children's reading is appropriate throughout the primary school. Obviously the practical aspects will vary from age to age (nursery parents, for example, should be encouraged to borrow books to read to their children whereas eleven-year-olds will be more likely to take home books to read to themselves and to discuss with their parents). The theme running through the entire age range is that children should be encouraged to build up a 'reading habit'. Some secondary schools have now started encouraging parental participation in their child's reading to try to encourage older children to 'carry on reading'.

Organisation

There is no blueprint for organising parental involvement. The situation within each school and each class will be different. What is most important is for each school (or class) to devise some pattern of organisation that is suitable to them and that fits in with the needs and interests of the children, parents and teachers. It is important that you plan your project carefully. You will need to have discussions first within the school, and then with parents about what the project will entail, whether you will keep records, how you might keep it going once you have got it started etc.

Involving parents in the classroom relieves pressure on teacher time.

Introducing the idea to parents

Parents want the best for their children. They want to help them do well and so are interested in working with the school. If this is to be 'collaboration' between home and school, then it is vital that both sides see it as such and that parents are involved from the beginning. You will need to explain not only the practical aspects but also the background to parental involvement; why schools now realise the importance of parental collaboration and the positive benefits for children's reading.

Each school will have to decide what is the most appropriate way of introducing the idea to parents. The initial contact should probably be by letter. You might find it useful to have a 'reply slip' at the bottom for them to return so that you will know how many to cater for.

You will then want to organise a meeting, either for the whole school (possibly with a visiting speaker), or a series of smaller informal meetings, or a combination. Parents will have concerns about their child's reading, and about how they can best help. These worries are more easily voiced in a smaller informal group where they can be handled sensitively. This is particularly important if some of your parents are not confident in their use of English or in their abilities as a reader. You should stress that it is the parents' support and interest in their child's reading that is most important, and this is something that all parents can offer.

Even if the aim is that the whole school will be involved in a home/school reading policy it may be best to start with just one class or section of the school. In this way any teething troubles will be worked out and you will be able to show to the rest of the school and to parents how successful it can be.

Practical considerations

It is important that parents are clear about what you are asking them to do. It seems reasonable to suggest to parents that they spend ten minutes two or three times a week sharing a book with their child. Some schools ask parents to hear their children read, others encourage a wider view of reading which emphasises the enjoyment of reading. Parents are encouraged to read to their children as well as hear them read, and

Without guidance parents may try to 'teach' as they remember being taught themselves.

to talk about the books, what they are about and the authors and illustrators.

Some schools keep some record of parents and teachers comments about the books whilst others just encourage children to take home books to share (see page 00 for card).

Whatever method is used it is important to offer: *Guidance for parents on how to help with reading* (see page 209 for the list of Dos and Don'ts).

Current thinking about the teaching of reading, acknowledging the importance of reading for meaning as opposed to reading by word recognition and phonic decoding, must be explained to parents. If it isn't many parents will try to help their children to read in the rigid way in which they learnt. Nothing kills pleasure in reading more quickly than endless 'sounding out'.

Make sure you give parents plenty of practical advice. Explain to them that in the early stages of reading children will 'approximate' to the text, ie the children will be using a range of clues and that 'guessing' and 'making sense' are very good signs. Ask the parents to praise the child frequently as it is always better than getting cross (however difficult that may be on occasions). The parent and the child will need to find a time and place to share books that is suitable to both (ie not when either's favourite television programme is on!) Most important of all the parents should enjoy the books and be interested in their child's reading.

Some schools and organisations have made videos showing examples of children reading at home. One school organised a parents' meeting where the teachers acted out some 'Dos and Don'ts' for helping children with reading which proved very useful as well as a great deal of amusement all round.

Record keeping

You will need to decide if and how to record participation. The PACT scheme suggests the use of a book marker with plenty of space to record the title of the book, the date and comments from the child's parents or teacher about the book or the reading. This enables some dialogue between home and school. Alternatively, a little notebook or exercise book could be used. Parents may be unsure initially as to what comments are appropriate, but yours will provide a model for them to follow.

Organising the books

You will need to make sure that your school has enough books. The number of books read will increase enormously. You will also need to work out which books will be the ones to be taken home. As the purpose is to encourage children to enjoy books, it is important to make sure that the books are enjoyable and also that children have a certain amount of choice over the books they take home to read. Children should have the opportunity to take home favourite books that they know well, as well as books they are reading in school. Also let them take home books they would like to have read to them or to share with their parents.

Parents want to know how their children are doing in relation to others. If your school uses a reading scheme in which each book is numbered and coded there is bound to be pressure from parents for children 'to get on to the next book'. When this happens the 'enjoyment' side can quickly disappear. By offering children a choice, the competitiveness is minimised. It also gives teachers (and children) the opportunity to respond to a particular situation. For example, children who are anxious about their reading need to have books that they are confident that they are able to read.

Children are very perceptive about pressures from home, and giving them a choice enables them to choose books they can cope with.

If you have bilingual children in the school it is useful to build up a number of dual language books and books in the children's home languages that they can take home to read or have read to them. (See also Multicultural approaches page 161.)

Another idea is to have a collection of taped stories that children can borrow and listen to at home. These can be bought commercially or taped in school. Use a signal such as a bell to indicate when to turn the page.

Some funds will need to be put aside for replacing books that will inevitably get spoiled or lost. Covering books with tacky back or putting on plastic covers helps to prolong their life. Strangely enough far fewer books get lost than teachers expect, and the more successful the scheme the less lost and forgotten books there are.

Children should have the opportunity to take their favourite books home.

Organisation in the classroom

Involving parents in the children's reading should not give you an enormous amount of extra work. You will need to make a few adjustments to your classroom organisation, but these should be minimal.

Set aside a period either at the beginning or the end of the day for the children to choose their books. Allow plenty of time for them to read, browse, talk about and select their next books. It's useful to arrange the books so that the children know which books are where and can choose independently. Young children find choosing quite difficult (it is something that has to be 'learnt'). It is helpful to have a particular shelf or box of well-known books

You will need to allow plenty of time for children to choose which books they wish to take home.

that you can guide children to if they are having difficulty. It is also useful to have bookmarks saying things like 'Please read this book to your child', or 'This is a favourite book' to pop inside appropriate books to act as a message to parents. You can get the children to make these.

You will also need to provide some kind of bag for children to take their books home in, either heavy duty plastic bags, or drawstring bags that have been made in school (by teacher, parents, helpers or the children themselves).

It is important that if parents are writing comments about their children's reading that you respond to them. It is unrealistic timewise to do this every day and most teachers (and parents) settle into a routine of writing comments two or three times a week. This can often be done while the children are browsing and changing their books. Take the opportunity to talk to the child concerned about the book she is reading at the same time. These comments provide a record of the child's reading, and can be added to when the teacher hears the child read.

Keeping it going

Objectives

To maintain parents' involvement in reading with their children.

Level of development

Throughout the school.

Organisation

Most schools find that at the beginning there is a great deal of interest from parents and teachers in supporting children's reading. Even with the best will in the world, however this interest flags. It is important to organise a series of activities that act as a reminder of the importance of home/school reading. These can be physical reminders such as bookmarks, badges, or balloons emblazoned with a reading motto like 'Reading is fun'. Meetings and book events can be organised about one particular aspect of reading. For example, one theme could be 'Advice on choosing the right book for your child'. Representatives from the local library and/or bookshop could be invited to advise parents. Informal advice sessions are also useful as parents always have questions to ask about their child's reading. A tremendous amount of support can be gained from other parents who will say things like: 'Oh Tracy was like that last year but now I can't stop her reading.'

Badges will help to spread the idea that reading is fun around the playground.

Problems and difficulties

Many of the difficulties that teachers envisage in a home/school reading scheme do not materialise. Often teachers feel that parents are not interested in their children's progress at school, but this is generally not the case. The majority of schools are surprised and impressed with the high level of parental involvement. This is particularly true when there is a high level of interest and commitment from the teachers, and the school.

Inevitably though, it is not all plain sailing and some problems are bound to arise, often connected with parents' expectations about their children or about what is involved in reading. You will need to work out some kind of procedure for discussing problems with parents, as it is very difficult to talk to one parent at the end of the school day while trying to manage a class of children as well. It might be appropriate to have the language post holder (or person responsible for home/school liaison) available at a certain time to talk to any parents with problems.

There will be a small number of

children whose parents cannot be involved, for one reason or another. You will need to make provision for them to receive extra reading practice within the school. By using ancillary workers or volunteer reading helpers to work with these children, every child will be able to get extra adult support for their reading.

Long term assessment

The overwhelming feeling from schools which have set up programmes is that there are very positive benefits to be gained in involving parent in their child's reading. Where the school actively works to maintain interest, it is seen by children, parents and teachers as a vital part of primary education, and one which brings all parties closer together.

Some schools have felt that it has been so successful that they have moved on into involving parents in other areas of the curriculum, for example, maths. Others have extended this support to 'weekend assignments' where the family is involved in something related to the child's work in the classroom. In one school, for example, the parents and children worked together finding trademarks for a class project on heraldry. In another school the children were asked to collect mementoes from the 1940s for a project on the Second World War.

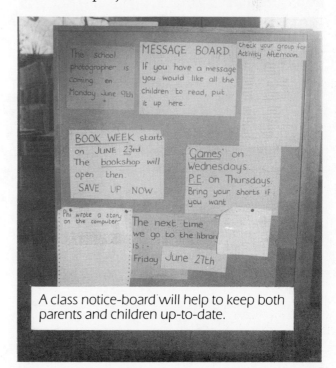

A class notice-board will help to keep both parents and children up-to-date.

Resources

Young Fluent Readers Margaret Clark, Heinemann (1976)

Language Learning and Education Gordon Wells, NFER-Nelson

The Foundations of Literacy Don Holdaway, Ashton Scholastic (1979)

Parental Involvement in Children's Reading K Topping and S Wolfendale (Eds), Croom Helm (1985)

Read! Read! Read! some advice on how to help your child Centre for Language in Primary Education, ILEA (1985)

PACT: home-school reading partnerships in Hackney Hackney Teacher's Centre, ILEA (1984)

Children and Parents Reading Alvin Jetts, Home and School Council, Sheffield (1984)

Children and Parents Spelling Alvin Jetts, Home and School Council, Sheffield (1985)

Involving Parents in the Teaching of Reading: some key sources Division of Education, University of Sheffield (1985)

Assessing books

Assessing books

INTRODUCTION

Sue Pidgeon has been teaching since 1970 in primary schools in the London area. For the past two years she has been one of two ILEA reading advisers. She is now a lecturer in primary education at Goldsmith's College.

Every day new children's books come on to the market. You just need to compare what you were offered at home and school as a child with the choice available today to get a feel for the change. With such a marked increase in publishing children's books in the last 20 years it is difficult, if not impossible to keep up with them all. So how can you assess which books to offer to children?

Along with a change in attitude to reading has gone a change in thinking about the books children 'learn to read' on. In the past the contents of these books was not considered important as children were expected first to 'master the mechanics of reading' and only later to understand and enjoy what they were reading. These books reflected the different approaches to reading. If it was the phonic approach then the books would be something along the lines of 'Tom Tit Tot was not a dot for a tot of shot.' If it was word recognition and building up vocabulary then the text would be something like 'I see Kitty. Kitty sees Mother. I see Mother. Kitty sees me. Do I see Kitty? Do I see Mother?' These were not very enjoyable books, nor was there much of a story. Now it seems strange that at the early stages of reading when it is important that children see the pleasure and purpose of reading, they were given books that had neither.

The work done by Frank Smith, the

Goodmans and others show that right from the beginning of learning to read, children try to do what a 'reader' does: they try to make sense of what they are reading. Therefore the books that children read are a part of the process of becoming a successful reader, and can help or hinder them. The reading process is the relationship between the reader and what they are reading, or more accurately, between the reader and the writer. The reader attempts to understand what the writer is writing about. The easiest books to read are those where the reader and writer share common knowledge of the subject and the way the book is written; the most difficult are those where the reader and writer diverge. This may be because the reader does not share the writer's knowledge of the subject matter. For example, I could read a book about astrophysics but I would have enormous difficulty understanding it because I know very little about the subject. It may be because the language used is not familiar to the reader, or it may be because the text does not conform to the reader's expectations about the structure. For example, certain modern novels are more difficult to read because they defy the conventions of the form of the novel.

Children also have to contend with all these factors when they are reading. The books that are easiest for them to read are those that fit in with their expectations about the language and structure of stories, and where they are interested in the subject matter.

Children build up a knowledge of books through reading and being read to. Prior to reading themselves children learn an enormous amount about books by having books read to them. Bedtime stories have always been acknowledged as being 'a good thing' but only recently has it been realised that they give children the basis to start reading themselves.

It is through being read to that children build up an understanding of what to expect in books, the language, the way a book works (moving through from front to back, left to right etc) the way stories work, and that they can relate what happens in their own lives to what happens in books. Through being read to, children learn that books are enjoyable and they soon choose favourite books that they like to have read again and again.

For children to build up a broad knowledge of books, they need to read and have read to them as wide a range of books as possible: non-fiction and fiction; fantasy and fact; traditional tales from different cultures and stories based in the real world; books they know well and books that are new to them; books to look at and books they are currently reading. Just as adult readers enjoy a variety of reading materials: magazines, newspapers, books to browse through, books to look things up in etc, children need a similar range.

The easiest books to read are those which use predictable text.

What to look for in books

Objectives

In assessing books for children our aim is to provide books that children can read and want to read. It is the books that encourage children to want to read, not the process itself and so we want to provide books that are enjoyable and readable.

Level of development

Throughout the age range.

Organisation

The enjoyment of books is such an important part of learning to read that teachers must try to provide books that both stress the pleasure to be gained from reading and are books that the children *can*

read. How can we assess and select from the enormous range available?

The first and most important criterion for choosing books is whether children enjoy them and the second is whether they are well written and illustrated. Although there is only a small number of books that really fulfil both these criteria (and have thus become universal favourites such as *Rosie's Walk, Where the Wild Things Are, Titch, The Very Hungry Caterpillar* and *Not Now Bernard*) there are very many more that children enjoy reading.

As a very rough rule of thumb the best way to assess books is to read them aloud to children. It soon becomes apparent if the book is enjoyable and if it is well written. If you have to elaborate the text to make it comprehensible, then the book will be difficult for a child to read.

Certain aspects of writing can help or hinder the reader, particularly at the early stages of reading when children are struggling to use all the cueing systems available to them. It is vital that the books support them. The easiest books to read are predictable ones; the most difficult are the ones that confound their predictions and offer no support.

The best way to assess books is to read them aloud to children.

The language of the book

Through being read to children build up expectations about the language of books. They know that book language is different from spoken language, and they expect it to make sense and to tell them what is going on in the book they are reading. The language helps the reader to predict and supplies support for their understanding. (For example the reader only has to read 'Once upon . . .' to know the rest of the phrase.)

Some books for early readers make the mistake of simplifying the text on the assumption that this will make it easier to read. Unfortunately it sometimes makes it more difficult as it removes the words that establish the causes and connections. Look at this example which has been rewritten to simplify it:

Original:
Chocolate was Jamie's favourite food. He would often sit at his desk and daydream about what he would buy when the school bell rang and he could rush round the corner to Mr Parker's store.

Rewritten:
Jamie liked chocolate. He liked to dream about chocolate. He would daydream at school. He bought his chocolate from Mr Parker's store.

In fact the second example is more difficult to read because the connection between the pieces of information is vague. Prediction is therefore more difficult as the reader is left to infer the reasoning. When assessing books it is important to see if the language of the text 'flows' or if it is unnaturally stilted, and difficult to read.

Vocabulary

How important is a structured vocabulary to the early stages? It is certainly true that the easiest books to read are predictable, and repetitive, but being repetitive does not necessarily mean limiting the text to a few words. Many good stories and rhymes repeat the vocabulary as part of the story without becoming contrived or losing the sense. Compare for example, these two extracts.

'Here is a wood. Here is a path. Here is a house.'

'In the dark dark wood there was a dark dark path. And up that dark dark path there was a dark dark house . . . .'

Both examples repeat the vocabulary but the latter uses the structure of the rhyme to let the language repeat itself naturally, thus making it more interesting and enjoyable to read.

Research done on repetition shows that there is a high level of repetition naturally in any piece of text. This is because a small number of 'key' words have to be repeated to keep language (all the connecting words for example) and also because the words that are relevant to the subject matter of the

63

piece will be repeated naturally. For example, if it is a story about a princess there will be a high level of repetition of words relating to her, to the palace, the King and Queen etc. Too much contrived uniformity of vocabulary will make a book boring.

The structure of the book

As most books read to children contain stories, they come to expect an element of story in the books they are reading themselves. Stories have a powerful influence on children, and they know a lot about them. It is important that children see the connection between the stories read and told to them and the books they are reading in school. Some of the books that are produced as early readers do not have any sense of story, and this can be quite disorientating for the readers. Some early books just have one or two words on the page and are really labelling books (eg 'the cat', 'the dog'). When toddlers first encounter picture books, they start by pointing at items on the pages and labelling them (in much the same way as they do when they start talking). Very soon they start to make up stories to go with the pictures. When children are old enough to start to read they are beyond the labelling stage. Similarly other books start by trying to tell a story using just one word (eg 'here').

Both of these approaches can give a misleading impression of what is involved in reading, and do not support the child's expectation that the book will tell a story. The best books are stories that from the earliest stages give children the incentive to read on.

Illustrations

Pictures provide an important clue for children when they are reading, particularly at the early stages. It is therefore useful to assess whether the pictures actually illustrate the text. All teachers will be familiar with the child who looks to pictures for some clue and gives completely the wrong word, either because the essential piece of information has been left out of the picture or is so badly drawn that it is impossible to get any help from it. The

illustrations on each page should complement the text given there.

Illustrations can make or break a book.

Interest level

Children need books that appeal to them at their age and stage of development. These will be stories based in the real world as they deal with themes of common interest to children as well as fantasy and traditional tales. Most books broadly speaking appeal to the age group they are aimed at, and match interest and reading level.

Occasionally there are books that children are very interested in but that are beyond their reading level. Few information books, for example, match interest and reading level suitably to a young reader, (see page 69 for further discussion on information books).

The other typical mismatch is when children are very interested in a particular series or character, usually on television, and want to read the book which is well above their reading level (and often quite difficult to read as well). A recent case in point is *Thomas the Tank Engine*, which became immensely popular through the television programmes with five to seven-year-olds, but when children wanted to read the books they found they were well beyond their reading and understanding capabilities. In both these situations the best solution is to read the books aloud to the children, and discuss why they may be difficult and why they may not be suitable.

It is sometimes difficult to match the interest level with the reading level for children at either end of the reading spectrum. The poor reader may be confined to 'baby' books and the 'good' reader to books with an interest level way beyond their intellectual capacity.

It is important in any class or school to have a large range of books that appeal to a wide level of abilities. It is generally accepted that classes may have up to a five year span of ability and yet the children will, on the whole, be interested in the same things, and enjoy many of the same books.

Many good readers get pushed on to read books way beyond their understanding and that very quickly takes away the enjoyment of reading. There are so many children's books available that it should be possible to find books suitable to each child's age and interest level.

By stocking a large range of books in your classroom you will ensure that there is something to suit each child's age and interest level.

Print

Schools used to place much importance on the type of print used in books children were reading and the size of the letters. Some series only used lower case letters,

Children are used to seeing a variety of typefaces.

some did not use any punctuation, others introduced capital letters gradually. However research on children's writing development shows that working out the relation between letters is part of their developing knowledge of print. Children are aware of all the print that surrounds them: the print on advertisements on television and in the street, shop names, signs, names on packets, tins etc and this is written in a variety of different print styles. Children notice this and can hypothesise from it for example that 'A', 'a' and '*a*' are all the same letter. So they are quite prepared to see capital and lower case letters in their books. In fact, it can be quite misleading to children to pretend that there is only one way of writing 'a'.

Another aspect of print in books is the way it is laid out. There seems to be an idea that it is easier to read short lines but when it is written
like this it is very difficult
to make sense of
it because the lines are short
and your eyes expect them
to each be a sentence.

However, it is equally true that very long lines of text can confuse the eye and be rather daunting to the young reader.

Poor line breaks can make it quite difficult to keep the sense when your eyes are not drawn on. Good readers scan forward and back to help them make sense of their reading. Sometimes the layout of the book can make this more difficult and it is worth bearing this in mind when assessing books.

Evaluating existing stock

Objectives

The preceding section looked at aspects of books that can make them more or less suitable to young readers. No one would possibly expect teachers to go through all their books assessing them for language, story, interest etc, but as you are reading books aloud or hearing children read these are factors you should be aware of. Certainly when choosing new books these are points to bear in mind.

Level of development

Throughout the primary range.

Classroom organisation

Now we are more aware of the important part that books play in learning to read, we must look more closely at what we are offering children.

Assessing reading schemes

For many years reading schemes have provided children with books to 'learn to read'. Some of these books have been wonderful; some have been deadly dull. Some have turned children on to reading and others have turned children off. When reading schemes were introduced they were innovative and provided books for children to read at a time when there were very few children's books. With the wide range of books available today it is possible to be more selective and to choose only those books that will stand up in their own right as enjoyable and readable. Within this selection will be books from schemes, from series as well as published children's books.

When looking at reading schemes it is worth bearing in mind certain points. Firstly, there is no evidence to suggest that children learn to read better or more easily using any particular reading scheme. In fact although many millions of children have learned to read very successfully using reading schemes, there are also millions of children and young adults who have also used reading schemes who do not see any pleasure or purpose in reading, do not choose to read and are not very competent readers. Secondly, as discussed earlier in this chapter, simplifying the text can make books more difficult to read and render them pretty meaningless. Many early books in reading schemes still fall into this trap, and give the impression that reading is about word recognition and not understanding.

Thirdly, reading schemes can take away the element of 'choice' in reading (see next section) and can emphasise reading as a competitive activity. Furthermore, as the 'reading scheme' books are part of 'reading at school', they can deny children the opportunity to read for themselves some of the best written and most enjoyable children's books and serve to emphasise the divide between home and school. School is a powerful source for recommending books to children and yet the scheme books are not available in bookshops and libraries.

Having said all that, reading schemes have simplified the task of selecting books. No one should suggest either that teachers should unwillingly throw out reading schemes (not to mention the fact that few schools could afford to do this) nor that you should spend hours attempting to assess the books. You can, however, use the knowledge you have about children's books to extend and supplement their selection to offer children a range of enjoyable and readable books.

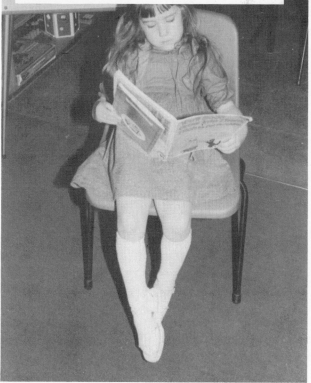

Use your knowledge of children's literature to extend the reading scheme books in your classroom.

Grading the books

Objectives

Is it necessary to grade the books? Obviously it is useful to have an idea of the reading level of the books available, but there is no infallible way of doing this. Using the criteria mentioned earlier, you can very roughly grade any book you come in contact with. There is no need to be too rigid about this as children will choose books they are interested in and can read.

Level of development

Throughout the primary school.

Classroom organisation

In the sixties and seventies 'Readability Formulae' were developed to assess the difficulty of books and they remain very popular in America. These look at the number of syllables in every so many words and the length of the sentences and grade the text accordingly. Unfortunately books are not written to a 'formula' and there were some bizarre results, for example *War and Peace* was designated easier to read than a Dick Bruna book! They also tend to favour books with a simplified text, which as was discussed earlier, are not necessarily the easiest books to read.

Publishers are aware that teachers are looking for a wider range of books and are now selling selections of published paperbacks that are appropriate for certain levels. Charts listing books in graded levels of 'difficulty' are also available, see page 71.

It is not necessary, though, to regard any one assessment as absolute or to follow it slavishly. Nor is it necessary rigidly to colour code books (see page 8). With your knowledge of children's books you will find that you don't always agree with other people's way of grading books. Guides are useful however to give a rough idea of the level of difficulty of the books that are available.

To help children make their selection the books can be loosely arranged in the classroom. For example you may find it helpful to put all the very well-known books that are easy to read on a particular shelf, or to put the books you will read aloud (or which very competent readers may choose to read) in another place.

Are reading ages necessary?

It may seem tempting to try to assess children's reading ages using one of the many tests available in order to match them to the books. Again, a reading age is not an absolute measurement. Each test emphasises one aspect of reading and there can be sharply diverging scores for the same child on different tests. Each teacher develops their own strategies for assessing how children are doing (see chapter on Hearing children read, page 73). With experience they are able to say things like 'she's reading at around the level of a seven year old', and these are just as useful as a reading age. Where books suggest the 'reading age' they are suitable for this can be used as a rough guide to the fact that the book is around the interest level and reading level of that particular age.

Follow-up

In addition to looking for books that are enjoyable and readable it is also important to examine presentation. Children these days are exposed to very high quality design in their television programmes and advertisements, videos and computer games. If books are going to compete with these for children's time and attention they must be well presented with a high standard of design and illustration.

Information books

Most of this chapter has dealt with fiction in the classroom, but it is important to consider non-fiction as well. Many children enjoy information books and would like to read them, but often find them difficult. There are two reasons for this. Firstly there are few children's information books that are both enjoyable and readable, and secondly children do not have very much knowledge of how information books work.

When looking at information books it is worth considering them in terms of language, vocabulary and interest level. Some are so simplified that they give the reader no information; others jump from subject area to subject area or use very technical language. Some information books now are written with a story structure that is already familiar to children, for example *The Life of the Stickleback* and these are easier for children to read.

The other side of assessing information books is to ensure that children know how an information book works. The best way to do this is to read them aloud. In this way you can find out how useful the book is, and it also allows the children to build up knowledge about information books: about contents pages, section headings, diagrams, and captions under pictures. By talking about the way information books work you can prepare the children for tackling them themselves.

The balanced bookshelf

Another important aspect of assessing books is the content. Books are a powerful source of knowledge and ideas so it is important that the books available to

The books in your classroom should reflect the multicultural nature of our society.

children put across ideas that are morally and factually sound. Children are being educated in a multicultural society and yet many books available hardly acknowledge this. You should certainly remove any racist or sexist books from your bookshelves if you have not already done so. When buying new books it is worthwhile building up the selection of multicultural books. These should be traditional stories from different countries and cultures, books about different festivals and stories that reflect the children's lives in the Western world and show minority groups and women in positive roles. Stories are relevant to all children; prejudice is based on ignorance and there is no need for children to be ignorant about the lives and cultures of their contemporaries (see also chapter on Multicultural approaches to reading).

The children's role

Choosing books is part of reading. We want children to see the pleasure and purpose in reading to be independent readers. This means that they must have some control over the books they are going to read. When assessing books for children it is important to leave them opportunities to choose, and their choices will help you to know which are the books they enjoy. Different techniques you can teach to children on how to go about selecting books are discussed on pages 126 and 143.

The choices children make tell us a great deal about themselves as a reader. A child who sees that reading is something to enjoy and understand will choose a book she can read, and this is something we want all children to be able to do.

Resources

Learning to Read with Picture Books (3rd Edition) Jill Bennett, The Thimble Press (1985)

Picture Books for Young People 9–13 (2nd Edition) Elaine Moss, The Thimble Press (1985)

A Choice of Stories Jill Bennett, School Library Association (1982)

Read with me: an apprenticeship approach to reading Liz Waterland, The Thimble Press (1985)

Individual Reading Sets Jill Bennett, Liz Waterland, Elaine Moss and Irene Yates, Scholastic Publications, Westfield Road, Southam, Nr Leamington Spa, Warwickshire CV33 0JH

Individualised Reading Cliff Moon, Centre for the Teaching of Reading, School of Education, University of Reading

Kaleidoscope Reading Sets Seven sets based on Cliff Moon's 'Individualised Reading Stages', Books for Students, 58–64 Berrington Road, Sydenham Estate, Leamington Spa, Warwickshire CV31 1BR

Kaleidoscope Book Boxes Four boxes selected by Michael Jones, Books for Students

Puffin Library Bookshelves Six sets from the Puffin lists, Oliver & Boyd

Cascades Library Pack Selected from Collins Publications, Educational Sales Office, Collins Publishers, PO Box, Glasgow G4 0NB

Hearing children read

Hearing children read

INTRODUCTION

Keith Topping is the Director of the Kirklees Paired Reading Project. He is the co-editor (with Sheila Wolfendale) of *Parental Involvement in Children's Reading*, the major work in the field, and author of many works on reading and other subjects in education.

Everyone agrees that listening to children read and reading with children is important. It is through the process of reading that children learn to read.

Traditionally, primary school teachers have assumed sole responsibility for teaching children to read. Occasionally they sent reading scheme books home with a general encouragement to parents to 'hear the child read', but on the whole it was felt that the teaching of reading should be left to those who knew how – the teachers. Teachers were thus faced with the impossible task of trying to listen to each of their children read on a regular basis, without creating gaps in their coverage of

other areas of the curriculum. The amount of time the teacher could devote to listening to each child read was insufficient to give each child the reading practice needed.

The attitude of schools towards involving parents has changed dramatically over the past 15 years. Parents are now actively encouraged to be involved in a whole range of activities both within and outside the school (see chapter on Involving parents). Other adult volunteers, such as old age pensioners, are also coming into schools to work with children.

Additionally, more and more schools are experimenting with using children as tutors for other children. In some cases this involves older children, either from the same school or from another one, helping younger and less competent readers. However, the more able readers within one class can effectively tutor the less able readers within the same class. This combination tends to be easier to organise. Children involved in such 'peer tutor' projects usually enjoy the experience, and the tutors often improve their reading skills *more* than the tutees.

Advantages of using non-professionals

Non-professionals have more time available to work with a child in a regular and frequent one-to-one situation. Thus the children simply get more practice at reading and more direct feedback than they would in any other situation.

Another valuable component of this type of tutoring is the 'modelling' aspect. There is often much positive demonstration of correct behaviour by the tutor which the child can copy (consciously or otherwise). This will particularly apply where some form of 'reading together' is used.

The reinforcement factor is also highly significant. Even teachers who regard themselves as very positive in their approach usually criticise children more frequently than they praise them. Non-professional tutors have the time to give much more praise and other social rewards than teachers, although they do have to be coached in how and when praise should be given.

Training is clearly crucial. Without it, the untrained tutor may give children more reading practice, but it is important that the practice is *positive*, ie is practice at reading *successfully*, and that the child finds it enjoyable.

The level of development of the *tutors* must also be considered. Where the literacy level of the tutor is low, the readability of the materials involved must be controlled to that level. If this is not done, the tutor's inability to correct mistakes will only cause confusion and frustration for the tutee.

A great number of methods and techniques for 'hearing' children read have been developed; however, not all of them have been shown to be effective. Only techniques which have been clearly

Peer teaching allows you to assess informally the reading of both children at once.

described and well evaluated will be considered here. Included in this chapter are: guided listening, reading together, paired reading and pause, prompt and praise. Readers requiring comparative information about other techniques should consult *WHICH Parental Involvement in Reading Scheme?* (see Resources).

If you know the children are receiving their practice elsewhere, you will be able to devote more of your time to assessing their reading development and devising strategies to improve their performance. Informal reading inventories and miscue analysis are assessment procedures which, in a modified form, can easily be used in the classroom. However, assessment of children's reading should not only be of their ability to read aloud. Their comprehension and silent reading skills should also be assessed and monitored. Various ways of doing this, including the cloze procedure, are discussed in this chapter.

The teacher's role

By using non-professional reading tutors, you are not giving up the role of teaching reading. Instead you are using them to ensure that your children receive as much reading practice as possible.

When hearing children read in class it is important to be clear about motives. It is very easy to concentrate on the child's errors and fail to give sufficient praise and reinforcement for correct reading. When this happens the weak reader may come to dread the daily 'examination' of reading prowess (or lack of it). Research shows that teachers tend to interrupt weak readers more frequently than they do fluent readers, proportional to errors made. Furthermore, research shows that teachers often interrupt too soon, failing to allow the child time to self correct.

Making 'errors' while reading is normal. Adults do it all the time when reading complex texts. They are made at all ages and at all levels of reading ability.

It is important not to become too pre-occupied with word attack skills at the expense of 'meaning attack' skills. Some children learn to 'read' quite fluently but without comprehension. Rather than trying to analyse each of the child's errors it might be better to think of them as educated guesses as to the possible meaning of the text.

Guided listening

Objectives

There is good evidence that whether parents hear their children read at home is a major factor, if not *the* major factor, in children's reading development, irrespective of socio-economic status or intelligence. Thus, establishing a guided listening scheme (ie encouraging parents to listen to their children read) can only be to the benefit of the children.

Level of development

Guided listening can be used throughout the primary school, although it is most commonly used for younger children.

Classroom organisation

Decide which books you will use. Will you use reading scheme books, 'real books' or a combination of the two? It helps to provide plastic folders for water-proof transit. You will need a simple recording system, on which the parent can note the pages read and, if wished, their comments, so that you will be able to check the children's progress at regular intervals. The card on page 194 can be used for this purpose.

The amount of guidance given to parents by schools varies enormously. The better the advice and training the school gives, the more the children will benefit. It will help if you give parents a talk about good practice and provide a list of 'Dos and Don'ts' such as that given on page 209.

Parents are often confused about what to do when the child gets a word wrong. You will need to give clear and detailed guidance on this point. Tell the parents that they should encourage the child to guess at any words she can't read. If she is unable to, the parent should prompt her with the beginning sounds. If that still doesn't help, the parent should tell her the word and let her carry on reading. Remind parents that the experience should be enjoyable for the child. Endless sounding out of words should be avoided.

Providing an actual demonstration of bad and good practice helps enormously to show parents what is expected of them.

Reading together

Objectives

Reading together is a relaxing and enjoyable way for a child to acquire many of the skills of reading by imitation, while eliminating any fear of failure.

Level of development

Reading together forms a natural link in a child's development between the acquisition of spoken language and the acquisition of written language, between listening to stories and reading them independently. Although it is probably most appropriate for younger readers, it can also be used for those readers who wish to read books above their current level of independent readability.

Classroom organisation

Reading together quite simply means that the adult and child read aloud together. As with guided listening, the atmosphere should be relaxed and happy, with the child sitting close to the adult. The book should

be discussed before, during and after reading.

The adult should synchronize his speed, pacing and rhythm to that of child, thus providing the child with a continuous demonstration of correct reading including fluency, expression and attention to punctuation. Parents may need practice to learn how to do this properly. Many schools organise workshops in which the parents can practise reading aloud together.

When reading together, mistakes by the child can be ignored to a large extent, as continuity and context are far more important. An exception to this is where reading together is used as part of the wider 'paired reading' technique (see below).

Paired reading

Objectives

Paired reading is a technique of which reading together is one part. Children are allowed complete freedom in choosing their own reading material, irrespective of readability level. Clear guidelines are given regarding how much help should be given and when. The technique supports children in their transfer to independent reading aloud.

Level of development

Paired reading has been successfully used with age groups ranging from children aged six to middle aged adults. It is most often used with primary aged children, but the technique is useful for anyone wishing to attack texts above their current readability level.

Classroom organisation

Most children find the freedom of being able to choose their own reading material highly motivating. One of the effects of establishing a paired reading project is that the children will read far more books than they did before. You will need to ensure in advance that you have an adequate supply of reading materials. Will the children be allowed to choose from wherever they like? Will the school library be available? Will the children be able to use it on a daily basis? Is it acceptable for them to read books from home, or magazines or comics?

Paired reading works as follows. Again, discussion of the text is much encouraged. On difficult texts, the tutor and the tutee read aloud together, tutor adjusting to tutee's speed. The child has to read every word, but in the event of an error or difficulty on any word lasting more than five seconds, the tutor repeats the word until the child self-corrects, and the pair then carry on. Pointing to the words while reading them helps to ensure the child does not listen without also looking. Frequent praise should be given for correct reading and spontaneous self corrections.

When the child feels able to manage a section of text without the support of the tutor, the child makes a pre-arranged gesture or other signal (eg a tap or a nudge), at which the tutor must praise the child for taking the initiative and then become silent immediately. The child carries on reading aloud alone until an error is made or a hesitation of up to five seconds occurs. At this point, the tutor says the word for the child to repeat, then the pair *continue reading together* until the child again feels ready to read independently. Throughout the process the tutor should continue to praise the tutee frequently.

This is the original form of paired reading, and is the best evaluated technique in the United Kingdom. Very substantial gains in reading ability have been found in very large numbers of children.

Training the tutors

With paired reading it is important to train the tutors and the tutees in the technique.

As they will need practice in using the technique, it makes organisational sense to

Practice and feedback is an essential part of training.

train tutors and tutees together in the same meeting. It is useful to start the training session by giving a short talk about the aims and methods of paired reading. It is also useful to give tutors and tutees written information about methods to take away to remind themselves later (see page 195). The majority of the training session however, should be devoted to a demonstration of how the technique is to be carried out. The effectiveness of this may be increased if the trainees are previously given a humorous demonstration of how *not* to do it, which they may be able to relate to their own previous practice.

The tutors and tutees should then be given a chance to try out the techniques. This will enable you to check that they are proceeding correctly, and give further individual help where necessary.

Some kind of formal or informal contracting, verbal or written, will help to reinforce the commitment between tutor and tutee. Provide the pairs with record sheets for them to fill in (see page 194). This will enable you to keep track of their progress.

Peer tutors

Where you are using peer tutors for paired reading, you will need to consider their level of maturity, experience of co-operative work, and the sex balance in the group. A project set up during class time with the tutors and the tutees coming from the same class is the easiest to organise. In most classrooms you will find a sufficient range of reading levels for this to be possible. You may feel, however, that because of the level of maturity of your children, cross-age tutors would be more appropriate. If the tutors come from a different school the organisational side can be quite complicated. Decide whether the session is to be timetabled or arranged by negotiation between the pair.

When using peer tutors the means of controlling the readability of the material to the level of the *tutor* needs to be clear. You will need to take pre-existing relationships in the peer group into account when dividing children into pairs. Extra tutors will need to be appointed to cover absence, and parental agreement should be sought.

When using peer tutors it is important that the material used is within the reading level of the tutor.

Pause, prompt and praise

Objectives

As with paired reading, this method may seem at first sight to contain little that is new. Its effectiveness lies in the fact that it embodies a few simple precepts of good practice in a coherent 'package', which is easily understood and applied by parents.

Level of development

'Pause, prompt, and praise' was originally developed for use with children with particular difficulties and has been used in primary and secondary schools in this way. However, many teachers may feel that it has obvious wider applications.

Classroom organisation

Pause, prompt, and praise emphasises very frequent praise for correct reading. The praise is elaborated so that the child will be clear about what aspect of his performance is being praised. Usually children use books which are slightly above their independent reading level. Tutors can be taught to assess the readability of books (see page 68).

The child reads the book aloud to the tutor. When she makes a mistake, the tutor pauses for *at least* five seconds, to give the child time to self correct. If she does not self correct, the tutor helps or prompts her in one of three ways, according to the nature of the error made.

- If the mistake made sense, the child should be given clues about the way the word looks, eg you should ask about a letter sound which has been mispronounced.
- If the mistake did not make sense, the child should be prompted with clues about the meaning of the story, eg you should ask a question about the content.

- If the child says nothing, she should be encouraged to read on to the end of the sentence or to re-read the whole sentence in order to extract clues from the context.

In any event, if the child does not get the word correct after two prompts, she should be told the word.

Praise should be given when the child reads a sentence correctly, when she self corrects and when she gets a word correct after you have prompted her.

Informal reading inventories

Objectives

Informal reading inventories can be used by classroom teachers for assessment by observation. Their use stems from the assumption that every child has not only one reading age, but a distribution of reading age levels. A child's reading level is not only related to his reading ability, but also to the nature of the reading task in hand and a whole range of motivational factors.

Four levels of reading skill can be distinguished:

- Independent level – the level at which a child reads with fluency, understanding, enjoyment and accuracy, without supervision or help.
- Instructional level – at this level the material presents some difficulties to the child, but whilst some help is needed, much of the material is well within existing competence. It is at this level that children can benefit from direct teaching.
- Frustration level – the child is unable to cope with material at this level. She will make many errors, is slow, hesitant and

insecure, cannot really understand the text and tends to be easily distracted from it. The child will not benefit from reading at this level.

- Capacity level – at this level the child can understand 75 per cent of the material when it is read aloud by someone else. Thus it gives a measure of the child's understanding of the language in the material. Whilst this is useful to know it is difficult to test and is therefore rarely used.

Informal reading inventories (IRIs) were originally designed for use in a more clinical setting than the classroom. The child would be given a series of graded passages and his reading level on each piece would be tested. The teacher (or whoever was doing the assessment) would then be able to compare numerically (or quantitatively) the child's ability in various aspects, eg reading out loud in comparison to comprehension of the text. The version given here is modified so that it can be used on a day-to-day basis in the classroom. It will not give you a reading age (see page 69) for the child you are assessing, but will show you how he is coping with the material in the classroom, and give you a rough idea of how he compares with others in the same group.

Level of development

Using a suitable text, you can do an IRI at any stage or level, in this simple form.

Classroom organisation

Select a series of graded passages of text. These can be drawn from a reading scheme unknown to the child. Try to choose passages of high interest content. The length of the passages should increase as the difficulty increases. The results can be made more reliable by increasing the length or number of reading texts at a particular level,

but of course this becomes more time consuming.

Ask the child to read the passage aloud to you. It will be much easier to administer the IRI if you have your own copy of the passages being read. You will then be able to record what the errors are (and possibly subject them to miscue analysis – see page 84).

After the child has read each passage, question him about the content. Your questions should concern word meaning, matters of fact, as well as questions requiring extraction of the main ideas or concepts contained in the passage.

Count the total number of errors of accuracy, and work out amount of errors as a percentage of the total number of words in the passage. More than 5 per cent errors means the child is reading at frustration level and unable to cope. Between two and five per cent means he is reading at instructional level and can cope with teacher support. Less than two per cent means the child is reading at independent level and can cope with the material alone. The parallel criteria for comprehension are: Frustration: 30 per cent errors; Instructional: 10–30 per cent; Independent: less than 10 per cent.

By examining the errors carefully, you will be able to see where difficulties lie and decide whether those problems are to do with the mechanics of the reading process, the meaning of the text, or the conceptual development of the child. This kind of assessment says as much about the readability level of the text as the reading ability of the pupil.

After the child has finished reading the passage, ask him about the content. Don't limit your questions to the meaning of particular words or matters of fact. You should also check that the child understands the main ideas or concepts contained in the passage. Ask the child to predict what might happen next (and why). In the original form of the IRI the child's answers to these questions would then be converted into percentages, and the reading level could be worked out. For information on how to do this you should refer to the Resources list (page 95).

Informal reading inventories can be criticised on a number of grounds. It is not always clear what should be counted as an error. For example, if you counted all repetitions to be errors you might find the child reaching the frustration level very quickly. Similarly, if you count errors which are subsequently self corrected you will not get a true picture of the child's ability.

A related problem is that if you are trying to monitor the child's progress over a period of time, you will need to assess the readability level of the passages used very carefully. Supposedly similar graded readers can vary considerably, thus presenting a distorted picture.

Miscue analysis

Objectives

From 1964 Kenneth Goodman began tape-recording poor readers in order to analyse the mis-match between what the text said and what they read aloud. The mis-matches were termed 'miscues' (as opposed to 'errors'). 'Miscue analysis' then, far from being something mysterious, is a simply an observation of the patterns and strategies used by the poor reader to process the text.

The view of reading implicit in using miscue analysis is that the process is not merely one of decoding but is in fact psycholinguistic. In other words, as *talking* is producing oral language, and *listening* is

receiving spoken language, *writing* is the productive counterpart of talking and *reading* is the counterpart of listening. We speak and write in order to communicate; we listen and read in order to accept and understand others communicating with us. Reading, therefore, uses language to get at meaning. We always reconstruct the speaker's or writer's word in accord with our own experience. Much of what we see when we read is what we expect to see, or 'predict'. If our predictions prove to be wrong, we back-track and revise. Reading becomes a kind of guessing game, based on our own understanding of context.

It is qutie pissilbe to raed a txet wtih a

greta man y mistaeks becos we no hwat we expetc to rade; teh sense is ont afectid untl we distreb teh construction of the language moving by sentences words or about so not they correct are grammatically.

From this example it becomes obvious that what counts is interpretation, or reading for meaning.

Miscue analysis can show whether the poor reader is relying on decoding strategies of a phonic (sound) or graphic (visual) nature, ignoring contextual clues, in her struggle to get at meaning. It can also reveal the strategies used by the child who 'barks at the text' ie appears to be fluent but makes no progress beyond the instructional level of reading towards clear interpretation and understanding.

It is quite easy to apply a simplified form of miscue analysis in the classroom, and, although it takes time, it is fascinating to see the patterns that emerge, which often reveal the overall emphasis of the methods used by a school to teach reading! It need not be as complicated as it sounds and is well worth the effort involved.

This type of assessment attempts to gain insight into the child's mind and into the process of reading. The object of miscue analysis is not to test but to diagnose. The pattern(s) which analysis of the miscues reveals will show the strategies the child is using to attack new words and interpret meaning and this will assist in devising the kind of instructional material the child needs to overcome difficulties. Miscue

Tape-recording permits detailed miscue analysis later.

analysis shows up strengths as well as weaknesses.

Level of development

Miscue analysis can be applied to poor readers at any stage or age, using suitable, carefully chosen texts.

The text must always be difficult for the child to read so that it generates at least 25 miscues. It must not be longer than the reader can handle at one 'sitting' as he must read the entire story in order to absorb its continuity and its unified 'whole'.

Classroom organisation

After making an appropriate selection of text for the reader, prepare another exact copy for yourself upon which you will mark the miscues. As it is sometimes difficult to keep up with the child, using a tape-recorder is strongly recommended. In fact, this was an essential ingredient of the original format of miscue analysis, though it is possible to make your own informal general assessement without using one.

If possible, choose a short story that the child will enjoy reading rather than a piece of text that will give her the idea she is going to do another reading test. Give her a purpose for reading, eg she is to read the story aloud in order to retell it to you (the purpose is therefore to gain meaning for retelling). Advise that you will give her no help during the reading; she is to handle any problems however she likes (guessing, sounding, skipping, etc).

Whilst she reads, mark the miscues, using the code, on your worksheet. Afterwards, ask her to retell the story in her own words without interruption. You can ask open-ended questions to probe bits she may have missed but should not feed information she hasn't given you. Again, a tape of her retelling will be of enormous help to you, allowing you to listen and reflect in your own time.

The next task is to analyse the miscues. This can be as simple or as complicated as you wish.

The miscues in the text below have been analysed in very simple form. Once the worksheet is completed, listen to the tape and mark any miscues you may have missed. You can hear from the tape where the child has made a reasonable attempt to read for meaning and accuracy (positives) and also where she has carried on blithely, regardless of the fact that she is making only nonsense (negatives).

The table here is a simple analysis of the miscues in the given text.

Analysis of Miscues

Type of Miscue	Substitutions	Omissions	Insertions	Reversals	Corrections	Totals
Positive	33	6	5	1	12	57
Negative	22	12	1	—	—	35

Code for recording miscues:
Example sentence: It was the Sun's turn to shine on Sunday.

Type of Error	Coding	Example
Substitution	Underline and write in the word substituted.	It <u>was</u> the Sun's turn to shine on Sunday. *(were)*
Non-response	Dotted line under the word if reader waits to be prompted or asks.	It was the Sun's turn to shine on Sunday.
Insertion	Add additional word/s or part word added	It was the Sun's turn to shine on Sunday. *(Shine)*
Omission	Circle word/s left out.	It was the Sun's turn to shine (on) Sunday.
Pause	Stroke. Use when reader pauses for more than two seconds.	It was the Sun's turn to shine on Sunday.
Repetition	Mark the word/s repeated with a curved line.	It was the Sun's turn to shine on Sunday.
Correction	Write in original miscue and curved line with a c for self correction.	It was the Sun's turn to shine on Sunday. © Saturday

*Sentence taken from the beginning of the story which is analysed.

The Little Storm
from **More Stories to Tell**
(edited by Eileen Colwell)

It was the Sun's turn to shine on Sunday. On Monday the East Wind went out. On Tuesday, long before daybreak, St Peter was driving his sheep, the grey clouds, <u>out</u> of <u>their</u> fold. [© marks]

The Little Storm kept grumbling and muttering to itself. [©]

'When can I have turn?' it asked *[He / I / immediately]* impatiently.

'Well – maybe next Thursday!' said St Peter, smiling.

Sure enough, first thing on Thursday St Peter *[in-braid-ed]* unbarred the gates of Heaven and let the Little Storm out. *[Sure enough]*

Down went the Little Storm to earth, rushing and roaring. 'And who might you *[inquir-eed]* be?' inquired the weathercock on the steeple in surprise. [©]

'I'm the Little Storm! Come on, let's play a game!' And it seized the weathercock and whirled it around, faster and faster, until it was quite dizzy.

'Stop, stop!' screeched the poor *[Scratched]*

weathercock. But the Little Storm was off again. There were nine oleander trees *[Was / Ordinen tree]* growing in brightly painted tubs outside *[tubes]* the cafe in the market place. They stood *[Over the]* there bolt upright, one behind the other. *[down]*

Whoosh! – the Little Storm rushed up to them. Three, five, seven, eight, nine – they (were) all bowled over! The Little Storm was off again. [©]

There was an empty sardine tin lying in *[Sergin]* the gutter in St Martin's Row. It had been there for days. It must have dropped out of the dust cart. Whoosh! Up swept the Little Storm. <u>How</u> that can rattled! Ping! It hit the *[R]* wall on the right. Ping! It hit the wall on the left. Then it shot through a gateway. *[and]*

The Little Storm shot through the gateway too, and came to a garden where *[Come]* there was washing hanging on the line. 'Ha, ha, ha!' chuckled the Little Storm, tearing an apron off the line. Just then a woman came *[© Come]* with a laundry basket. 'Good gracious, where's my apron?' she thought in alarm, looking around for it. Where indeed? Why, it was right up in the plum tree, on the very top branch! But the Little Storm was off again.

87

You will have your own copy of the text on which to record the miscues.

'What weather!' thought the Mayor, [a]

coming out of the Town Hall. 'What

shocking weather!' Whee! The Little Storm

[Come] came roaring up and tore the Mayor's hat

from his head with one gust. [and]

[©] 'What weather!' thought the burglar,

creeping up to an empty house. He had

[was sped] [of] spied it out before the people who lived [©]

there were all away on holiday. 'What

wonderful weather,' thought the burglar,

[Could] [wind] 'no one will hear a window pane break in

[the smashing] [of] this.' And he smashed in the glass.

'What weather!' thought the policeman

[in directing] standing in Station Road to direct the traffic.

[in] However, there was no traffic to direct in

[this] weather; everyone was staying at home.

[through] Ah, here comes a hat, though. The

[and] policeman spread his arms wide to hold it

[when there] [©] up, but it was not the slightest use. The hat

took no notice of him at all.

'Stop!' shouted the policeman angrily.

'Stop!' Was it an echo? No, it was the

Mayor just turning the corner. 'Catch that

hat!' he shouted.

[Laughing] 'Ho, ho, ho!' laughed the Little Storm,

dancing along with the hat – one, two, three,

hop! The policeman ran after the hat, the

88

Mayor ran after the policeman. But then

[©] they all stopped running and dancing, lo

and behold, they were standing outside a

[the windows] house with a window open. The glass was

broken.

'What's all this?' said the Mayor.

'What's all this?' said the policeman.

And last of all – 'What's all this?' said

the burglar. He was just climbing out of the

[his lot] [when he looked] window with his loot when, much to his

surprise, he felt two strong hands grab him.

'Whooooo!' howled the Little Storm

and away it blew.

Then all of a sudden it noticed how [he] terribly tired it was. It whistled quickly around a couple of corners, but it wasn't such fun any more. It began to yawn [yane], ©'Aaaaaah!'

©'What, as <u>tired</u> <u>as</u> all that?' asked a voice₀It sounded|familiar [fam-iar]. And when the Little Storm looked up, it [was] saw the Sun pushing the grey clouds aside and beaming down cheerfully.

'Come along, home you go,' said the Sun.

Then the Little Storm took one jump and hopped up on to one of the clouds, and back it flew to the sky. St Peter was standing outside the gates of Heaven. 'Well?' he asked [Said]. 'How was it?'

'Wonderful!' sighed [Said] the Little Storm happily₀'I played|whipping tops [and] with the weathercock and⒤played|ninepins with the |oleander trees [olden tree]. I played football with the| ©sardine tin and hide-and-seek with the apron. I played⟨tag⟩ with the Mayor's hat⟨and⟩ I played [with] cops-and-robbers. Aaaaaah!'

[I] [in the] It snuggled down into its soft grey cloud₀half asleep already₀but murmuring

[you could.]
'When can⒤do it again?'

'Next Thursday, maybe,' said St Peter smiling. 'We'll have to see.' And he closed the gates of Heaven.

What can we learn from this analysis?

First, we must ask questions and study the patterns of the miscues.

Look at the substitutions. How much do the words look alike? How much do they sound alike? Is the grammatical function of the substituted word the same as that of the original (ie verb? adverb? pronoun?)

Next, look at the sentences containing miscues. Is the syntax (grammatical structure) still acceptable? Is the sentence still semantically acceptable – does it make sense? Has the child changed the meaning of the sentence?

In the example the child relies heavily on phonic clues and is unwilling to guess even though many of her substitutions are nonsensical. Visual punctuation clues are often misinterpreted, and this distorts the meaning. Though her repetitions and corrections show that she is struggling to process the print for meaning, basically she is attempting decoding accuracy at the expense of comprehension, and the meaning degenerates for her as the story progresses.

From the taped version of her re-telling, it is clear that although she can recall specific details, she is confused about the story as a whole. Her inefficiency may be a result of her concern for word-by-word accuracy, and this may be due to an over-emphasis on phonic and graphic strategies in the past. The child needs to learn to make judgements as she is reading ('Does this make sense?') and overcome her tendency to accept nonsense as she is reading.

What to do about miscues

The main types of miscue and their possible causes are shown below:

Possible difficulty . . . may lead to . . .	Miscue
Child unable to decode Lacking confidence in prediction Concept outside child's experience	Refusal
Reading fluently with eyes ahead of voice/re-processing text simultaneously Good understanding of text Poorly written material	Acceptable substitution, ie wrong word, same meaning, eg Dad for Father
Poor decoding skills Low level of understanding Poorly written text	Unacceptable substitution, ie wrong word, wrong meaning
Reading fluently with eyes ahead of voice/re-processing text simultaneously Poorly written text	Insertions and Omissions
Trying to understand confusing syntax or style Trying to understand ambiguous meanings Misleading lay-out of text	Pauses, self-correction or repetition
Low level of understanding Misleading lay-out of text (eg with pictures placed in awkward position between words)	Inappropriate rises or falls of intonation

Only intervene during the reading at instances of refusal or unacceptable substitution.

- If the text is too difficult, give the child another.
- If the child substitutes a special noun, tell her the word.
- If the word is outside the child's experience, ask what she thinks the word should be, what she thinks fits the meaning. If the word she offers is an acceptable substitution, accept it, and tell her the word she refused, pointing out that it means the same.
- If the child finds the word too difficult to decode, but it is within her experience,

tell her to have another go at it from the begining of the sentence. Ask the child what the word might be, draw attention to its initial sound and to known syllables within the word. If she still can't get it, tell her the word.

There are problems with using miscue analysis. As with any form of assessment you can only make an informed guess as to the nature of the error the child has made, since what you observe may not correspond to what is going on in his head. When 'attacking' a difficult word the child might apply a variety of strategies, not always in the same sequence. None of this will be obvious, however, if in the end the child only verbalises his final attempt. The results you obtain from the miscue analysis will therefore have to be looked at in relation to the other informal assessments you have made.

Follow-up

Do not neglect to feed back the information derived to the child being assessed. Even quite young readers may benefit from a simple and clear description of how their reading seems to be going wrong, or at least of how it is less efficient than it might be. Some children may well prove able to respond to such information, particularly if you can suggest simple strategies with which they might experiment to see whether improved reading efficiency results. For example if the child consistently fails to use contextual cues, it is worth discussing with her how they might be used.

Comprehension

Objectives

Oral reading is mainly useful as a means of fostering more effective silent reading. If it is difficult to assess a child's interaction with the text when reading aloud, it is almost impossible when she is reading silently.

The traditional way of testing for comprehension, with the teacher setting interminable questions on the text for the child to answer after reading it, makes considerable demands on memory and also runs the risk of taking much of the enjoyment out of reading. There is evidence to suggest that a child's ability to understand a text is increased if that text has a high proportion of frequently used and well-known words, if the grammatical complexity is low, if the child has relevant background knowledge, and if the child has the opportunity to read the text more than once.

The techniques discussed in this section can be used for both improving and assessing comprehension. They can also be used to assess the readability level of the text provided. There is no point in trying to assess a child's comprehension of a text which is far too complex for him. On the other hand, use of 'comprehension exercises' as a teaching strategy rather than a testing strategy can aid the reading process.

Level of development

Comprehension exercises can be used at all stages, provided care is taken over the choice of text. They may be used before reading has begun; in fact, used with beginning readers, they greatly enhance the concept of story and print.

Classroom organisation

Choose a passage which evokes atmosphere, communicates ideas and presents good, figurative language. If you select a text from the book you are currently reading to your class you can focus on a part they will all enjoy and this is infinitely preferable to picking out texts in isolation and presenting them as 'tests' as the traditional form of comprehension exercise did.

To make the interaction between children, teacher and text most effective, employ talk rather than written language, giving the children the opportunity for structured discussion around the passage you have chosen.

Make sure that each child, or pair, has a copy of the text. First read it aloud to them, with them following it. Next, allow them to read the passage for themselves. With non-reading or beginning reading children use picture books, pictures, posters and comic strips. Pause and discuss the questions you have formulated with the children, guiding them backwards and forwards in the text to find their solutions.

The last stage is to let the children write answers to the questions, thus shaping what they have received from the text. Again, with non-readers or beginning readers, omit this stage or allow them to do their own pictures.

Formulating the questions

It is very easy to think of questions on a literal level, but it is much more difficult to think of questions that will require the children to 'read between the lines' or make a response or judgement about the text!

Take for an example, the passage quoted on page 94 from 'The Iron Man', (though one would normally use a much longer piece of narrative for class purposes, this is used merely for example).

Ask the children open-ended questions. This will encourage them to examine the text more closely than they would otherwise.

The kind of questions to ask at the Literal level are: What was the boy's name? What was he doing? More complex literal questions, involving re-organisation of the text: Where do you think Hogarth lived?

To answer questions at the Inferential level the child has to use clues and 'put two and two together': What kind of a boy do you think Hogarth was?

Evaluative responses could include: What kinds of feelings does the text stir in you? How do you think Hogarth feels?

Questions like these can lead the children to penetrate a text to a depth they would not normally approach. The oral aspects of the exercise allow them to listen to other viewpoints and perhaps change their own in the light of them, to consolidate their own knowledge of the text and to form some appreciation of its fabric.

This is not an instance in which the children can be 'right' or 'wrong'. Open-ended questions should lead to open-ended answers and the children should be encouraged to have confidence in their own feelings and ideas about the text. If they are 'miles out' they should be returned gently to the clues in the text and allowed to think it out again.

Follow-up

When the children are used to making a group interrogation of the text in this way, get them to make up their own questions on selected narrative passages to present to other members of the class. Such a task requires an absolute understanding of the passage in question and is totally demanding.

Cloze procedure

Objectives

The use of cloze procedure exercises enables you to measure the relationship between the reader's ability to anticipate meaning and her comprehension level. It assumes that if the reader understands the text, she will be able to make accurate predictions. It also tells you as much about the readability of the text for a particular pupil as about the reading ability of that pupil, therefore you have to be clear in your objective. Do you want to assess the child's ability to read the material you have set, or do you want to assess the material you have given the child to read?

Level of development

Cloze procedure can be used at any level of development and with any material currently being used in your teaching, so long as it is properly selected with your objectives firmly in mind.

Classroom organisation

There are two basic patterns for cloze procedure. One is to make regular deletions, for instance, delete every tenth, seventh or fifth word. (Obviously the more frequent the deletion, the more difficult comprehension will be.) The other is to make specific deletions where a particular reading difficulty has shown itself, for example a problem of vocabulary or structure – which may have been shown up by a miscue analysis.

- Select a text or an extract from a piece of current reading material of approximately 150 words.
- Decide on your strategy – do you wish to focus upon: vocabulary? key concept words? structural words? general understanding?
- Delete words according to your strategy, replacing with lines. It helps if the length of the line is proportional to the length of the word deleted.
- Until the children have understood the level of thinking necessary to work at cloze exercises let them work in groups on the exercises; discussion is crucial for them to develop their thinking. Obviously the children should be evenly matched for ability and your use of text and strategy should be based on recognition of those groups (in other words, you can't give all the children in the class the same material!). When they are familiar with the technique you can apply it to an individual reader to assess personal comprehension level.
- Analyse the information you have obtained from the results. Remember that you are operating in the field of accurate or intelligent prediction, not wild guesswork! As a general yardstick: 60 per cent or above correctness means that the reader has a high level of understanding. Below 40 per cent: the reader has very little understanding. Between 60 and 40 per cent indicates that the reader could understand the text with some support.

Example 1 Regular deletion, every seventh word

One evening a farmer's son, a _____ called Hogarth, was fishing in a _____ that ran down to the sea. _____ was growing too dark to fish, _____ hook kept getting caught in weeds _____ bushes. So he stopped fishing and _____ up from the stream and stood _____ to the owls in the wood _____ up the valley, and to the _____ behind him.

(This passage is from *The Iron Man* by Ted Hughes, Faber & Faber.)

Example 2 Specific deletion of vocabulary and function words

One _____ a farmer's son, a boy called Hogarth, was _____ in a stream that _____ down to the sea. It was growing _____ dark to fish, his hook kept _____ caught in weeds and bushes. _____ he stopped fishing and came up _____ the stream and stood listening to the owls in the wood further up the valley, and _____ sea behind him.

Follow-up

Basically the use of the cloze procedure as an assessment technique gives you choices. Whether the child is reading with complete understanding or not understanding at all, the questions you have to ask yourself are: In order to ensure that the child does not stand still but makes some development in reading, am I now going to change (a) the reading material to texts with a higher or lower readability level or (b) the child, by employing new strategies?

The use of cloze procedure as a teaching technique requires your constant intervention, so that you can assist the child in using all the clues that are in the text, as well as the previous knowledge or concepts that she may bring to the text in order to understand it. Group work of this nature, with considerable discussion, allows the child's thinking skills to develop towards the point where he is making an active interrogation of the text as he reads.

Children will be able to use the techniques learned by doing cloze procedure exercises when they read on their own.

Resources

Listening to Children Reading H Arnold, Hodder and Stoughton (1982)

Making Sense of It: miscue analysis during oral reading H Arnold, Hodder and Stoughton (1984)

The Early Detection of Reading Difficulties: a diagnostic survey with recovery procedures M Clay, Heinemann (1981)

Framework for Reading, J Dean and R Nichols, Evans Brothers (1974)

Reading Problems: identification and treatment (2nd edition) P Edwards, Heinemann Educational (1978)

Reading Miscue Inventory Y M Goodman and C L Burke, Collier MacMilland (1972)

Comprehension and Research Skills: an index of classroom resources D Gregson and S Thewlis, National Association for Remedial Education (1983)

Reading Comprehension Assessment: a cognitive basis P H Johnston, Newark, Delaware – International Reading Association (1983)

Approaches to the Informal Evaluation of Reading J J Pikulski and T Shanahan (Eds), Newark, Delaware – International Reading Association (1982)

Reading: tests and assessment techniques (2nd Edition) P D Pumfrey, Hodder and Stoughton (1985)

Cloze Procedure and the Teaching of Reading J Rye, Heinemann Educational (1983)

Parental Involvement in Children's Reading K Topping and S Wolfendale (Eds), Croom Helm (1985)

WHICH Parental Involvement in Reading Scheme? A guide for practitioners K Topping, *Reading* Vol 20, No 3, pp 148–156

Children and Parents Enjoy Reading Peter Branston and Mark Provis, Hodder and Stoughton (1986)

The Belfield Reading Project A Jackson and P Hannon, Belfield Community Council, Samson Street, Rochdale OL16 2XW

PACT: A handbook for teachers Pitfield Project, Hackney Teachers' Centre, Digby Road, London E9

Parent, Teacher, Child A Griffiths and D Hamilton, Methuen (1984)

Shared Reading Mary Greening and Jean Spenceley, Country Psychological Service, 5 Turner Street, Redcar TS10 1AY (The use of the term shared reading in this instance refers to reading together, as opposed to the meaning used in Chapter 3)

Paired Reading Training Pack (2nd edition) Paired Reading Project, Kirklees Psychological Service, Oldgate House, 2 Oldgate, Huddersfield HD1 6QW

Helping Children Read Roger Morgan, Methuen (1986)

Information on Pause, Prompt and Praise can be obtained from Kevin Wheldall and Frank Merrett, Department of Educational Psychology, University of Birmingham, PO Box 363, Birmingham B15 2TT

Bright Ideas Reading Activities Frankie Leibe, Scholastic Publications (1985)

How to Run Family Reading Groups C Obrist, United Kingdom Reading Association (1978)

Word Play: language activities for young children and their parents S Wolfendale and T Bryan, National Association for Remedial Education, Stafford (1986)

Word attack skills

Word attack skills

INTRODUCTION

Elizabeth Wood has had many year's experience as a primary school teacher. In 1975 she trained to teach dyslexics at The Dyslexia Institute and subsequently spent ten years giving private coaching to children with specific learning difficulties. She is the author of *Exercise your Spellings*, Books 1–3 and *Games to Exercise your Spelling* which complements the books.

The primary aim in teaching reading should be to give children an increasing ability to read what they want to read. A 'look and say' or 'sentence method' approach gives most children quick access to a limited range of reading material, but once their interest has been stimulated they will be ready to try all sorts of texts. They will want to read words they see around them, such as 'bus stop', 'in', 'exit' or the names of streets or shops, and they will also want to read any 'real' books that attract them. Make good use of this eagerness to read by teaching them some phonics; a child with a good

phonic knowledge will be able to tackle most words in the English language.

Using phonics for word attack

Whilst almost all children will use phonics to supplement their 'look and say' vocabulary, a few children who find the visual recall of whole words difficult will depend almost entirely on phonics to learn to read at all. If a child can learn the letters and combinations of letters that produce the 44 sounds from which all English words are built, he can tackle any word he wants to read.

Much of children's phonic knowledge will be picked up informally, whilst reading and being read to, and in casual conversation with you and their classmates. Rhymes, jingles and songs are particularly useful for this and it is unwise to embark on any formal phonics teaching programme until you have established the child's ability to listen to, recognise and enjoy the sounds that make up the English language.

A phonic teaching programme needs to be structured carefully. A child must build 'brick by brick' on what he already knows, travelling at his own pace, if his confidence, an important factor in the learning process, is to be maintained. Competition with more able children should be avoided because this can quickly undermine confidence. Try to give praise wherever possible and encourage children to improve their own performance and to have pride in their own achievements. Attempt to introduce all the activities in this chapter in a casual, informal and natural way. Draw incidental attention to sounds you hear and see, especially whilst looking at books together. Base your phonic work as far as possible on children's current reading interests, so that it does not become divorced from your overall reading approach.

The teaching of phonics should be developed beyond the teaching of simple sound/letter links and word building, through double sounds, sound blending and long vowel rules, to work with syllables. This will involve prefixes, suffixes and complex word endings such as 'tion' saying /shŭn/ and 'ture' saying /cher/. At this stage a child will need to have a well developed vocabulary if he is going to be able to pronounce words correctly, and pronunciation can be helped by learning about the usual position of the stress in a word.

Once again the more experience of reading, and being read to a child has, the more his ear will become attuned to hearing these subtle distinctions of language. The activities in this chapter will not teach reading on their own, but combined with regular contact with a wide variety of good

Sometimes it is advisable to eliminate the competitive element altogether, letting the children work as a team.

The games described in the following pages are versatile and can be adapted to serve many teaching points, and the needs of individual children. At the back of the book you will find cards and boards to play the games described in this chapter. These can be photocopied onto soft card then covered with sticky back paper. If you have access to a photocopier with enlarging facilities the board games should be enlarged from A4 to A3.

Aural work

Objectives

To help children to recognise individual phonic sounds aurally, by developing their awareness of the similarity of the sound at the beginning of words which start with the same letter.

Level of development

This will follow on from pre-reading listening activities.

Classroom organisation

- See that there are plenty of objects or pictures in the classroom starting with two or three different sounds. Get the children to name all the objects beginning with /s/, /c/, /p/ and so on. (Throughout this chapter // indicates the sound of a letter and ' ' shows the name of the letter being referred to.)

- Play an 'I Spy' game giving the initial sound (not the letter) to be found. Let the children have a turn at choosing what they can spy.

- Make alliterative sentences with the children such as 'clever cats climb on cars' or 'the Doctor's dog digs up the daisies', building on the children's suggestions where possible.

- Start a display table and ask the children to bring articles or pictures from home which start with one particular sound, for example, pictures of skyscrapers, sausages, soldiers, a six or a seven, and a saw. On the table there could be objects such as a saucepan, soap, a sock, a spoon, or a stamp. Display the written sound so that children recognise the sound/sight links. As soon as a few sounds have been learned begin to build words aurally. Ask the children to repeat a sound, eg /c/ and hold it until given the next sound /ă/ which is held until the next sound /t/ is given. Repeat, speeding up until they can identify the word. Build this activity into a word game: hide a picture card behind your back until the children guess the word correctly from the given sounds.

Follow-up

● Make up stories with the children including alliterative words using words from the display table. For example start a story about a soldier who lived in a skyscraper who had a hole in his sock. Let any child who wishes continue with the story bringing in new words beginning with /s/. Some children may add a lot to the story, others only a sentence or two. The structure of the story is not important at this stage. It is only the vehicle for the enjoyment of using a certain sound. If the story is written down the children can enjoy it as a class book.

● Get the children to practise listening for the end sound in a word. Ask them to discriminate between different endings: 'Would you lie down on a bed or a bell'? 'Would you put your cap on your head or your hen'?

● Get the children to pick the odd one out from three or four words, one of which starts with a different letter. When they have mastered this, do the same with the sounds at the end of words or with rhyming words.

● Introduce the concept of rhyming. Say nursery rhymes stressing the rhymes. Play a rhyming 'I Spy', eg 'I spy something rhyming with log (dog), hat (cat), fun (sun), pin (tin) and so on.

Sound/sight links

Objectives

To teach the link between individual sounds and both visual and written letters. Children must learn the correct way to *write* a letter as soon as it is introduced visually. This ensures that wrong formations do not have to be unlearned later on. Opinions vary as to the exact order in which sounds should be introduced, but if interest is to be sustained through the early stages, letters should be chosen which can quickly be combined to make three letter words and some sort of sentence, giving purpose to the learning of abstract sounds. Even though sentences will be very simple at this stage it is important to try to use names and objects of personal interest to the children. When 's', 'm', 'a', 'p', 'c', 'h' and 'i' have been introduced it will be possible to make up sentences such as 'Sam has a cap', 'Pam has a mac' or 'Pip has Sam's cap'. With 'n', 'o' and 't' a lot more sentences can be made.

Level of development

As soon as the children have grasped the concept of single phonic sounds, the linking of sounds to letters will come as a natural development. The degree of a child's pencil control will depend on the amount of manual dexterity he has acquired from previous physical activities such as ball play, painting and drawing. If a child has had rich experience he can start to write letters in a work book. Otherwise, give lots of practice first on a bigger scale, on drawing paper, on a blackboard or in a sand tray.

Children need physical activities such as drawing to develop the manual dexterity necessary for writing.

Classroom organisation

Letters should be introduced at a rate of about two or three a week. A useful order for teaching sounds would be 's', 'm', 'a', 'p', 'c', 'h', 'i', 'n', 'o', 't', 'e', 'd', 'k', 'l', 'f', 'r', 'b', 'g', 'u', 'v', 'w', 'j', 'qu', 'x', 'y', 'z'.

At this stage only short vowels should be introduced, and letters should be lower case. Try to stop the children adding an /er/ sound to letters such as 'm', 'n' and 't' because this will make word building more difficult later on. Keep the lips shut when saying /m/, the tongue against the top teeth for /n/ and the /t/ should be a short explosive sound.

The easiest way to teach 'y' is as another way of writing /ĭ/. Teach 'w' as /o͞o/ to keep the lips forward until the next sound is said, ie /o͞o/ /ĕ/ /t/. 's' is an easy sound/ sight link for children to learn, but whereas it hisses like a snake at the beginning of a word, by the end of a word the snake has often fallen asleep, and all we hear is /z/ as in 'has'.

The following activities are suggested for practice and revision:
- Put up wall charts showing a letter and matching picture or pictures. Some children will find that letters linked to a picture by a pictogram (where the letter echoes the shape of the picture) will be helpful (see Resources list, page 118). Each day reinforce the sounds already learned by reviewing the labelled items, getting the children to give the sound and the picture clue, eg /m/ for 'monkey'.
- Practise writing the sound. With the letter displayed on a flash card, the children practise writing the letter in the air, following the teacher's finger, (the letter will be in reverse for the teacher), and saying the sound as it is 'written'.
- Many children confuse the letter 'b' with the letter 'd' when they first learn them. A mnemonic which might help is to write the word 'bed'. If the letters are the right way round, a man can be drawn sleeping comfortably on the bed; if the letters are reversed 'deb' there is no room to lie down and the man would have to sit up all night.
- Some children will need not only to see, but to feel letters. Write the letter with a wax crayon on thin paper laid over a rough surface such as the back of a piece of hardboard. Let children feel the letter and get a tactile experience of it. Encourage them to say the sound as they feel the letter; this will give them a multi-

sensory experience of the sound/sight link: tactile, oral, auditory and visual. Involving these four senses will be of particular help to children with specific learning difficulties.

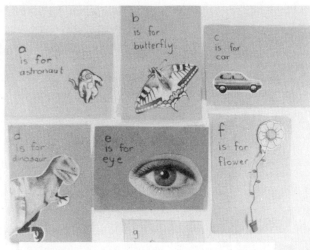

A display of letters and matching pictures will help to reinforce the sounds already learned.

Follow-up

- Let the children practise writing letters with a crayon or pencil, first with eyes open, then with eyes shut saying the sound as it is written, to reinforce the oral, visual and kinaesthetic links. Encourage the children to combine the letters to form words and/or simple sentences.
- Make a personal phonic reading pack for any child who is not keeping pace with the class, so that he can move forward at his own pace. Cut cards about 7.5cm × 5cm. Write a lower case letter on one side of the card and a picture clue to the sound on the reverse side. The child will look at the letter and try to remember the picture clue for that sound without looking on the back of the card. He will then give the clue picture then the sound, eg 'pig /p/'. In a classroom it will be easier if all the children have the same clues on their cards, but those with particular problems may need to choose their own clue pictures to stimulate their interest in reading. A boy with an overriding

interest in cars learned his sounds as /ă/ for Alfa Romeo, /b/ for Bentley and so on.

The pack should be checked through each day, and new letters only added when the sounds in the pack are known.

- Play the following matching games to give sound/sight link practice. Make one copy of the pictures and *two* copies of the alphabet letters on card (see pages 196 and 197) and cut up into two packs. Cut off one corner of the picture cards (if the letter on the bottom corner is not needed, this is the corner to cut away.) Make a copy of the picture sheets with letters to use as a check sheet. The letters and the number of pairs in the packs for each game, should be adjusted to the ability and stage of learning of the players, using between four and ten pairs for each player.
- To play **Find the letter**, spread the letter cards, face upwards on a table at one side of the room. The picture cards are stacked or held by the teacher at the other side of the room.

Each player takes a picture card and goes to the table to find a matching letter card. He takes the pair to his table, then takes another picture card. The winner is the player with the highest number of pairs at the end of the game. Each set of paired cards could be shuffled and put

Young children will enjoy playing 'Find the letter'.

into a rubber band to use as a pairing exercise the next day.

- To play **Picture lotto**, share the letter cards equally between the players, who put them face upwards on the table in front of them. The teacher, or a child, holds up a picture, and if a player has a

105

matching letter she puts her finger on the letter, and gives the sound and the picture, eg /b/ for butterfly. The first player to call gets the picture. The winner is the first player to match all her letters with a picture. This game can also be played with the players having the picture cards and the teacher or child the letters.

- To play the **memory game** (Pelmanism), you will need two pairs for each of the letters used, to give a fair chance of making a pair. Do not use more than 15 letters (30 pairs). Place all the cards face downwards on the table. The first player turns up one of the cards with a cut off corner (a picture card), then turns up a letter card to see if he can make a pair. If he does he keeps the pair and has a second turn, if not he turns the cards face downwards again in the same place and play passes to the next player. The winner is the player with the most pairs when the table is clear.

- **Match the picture** is a game for three or more players. The pack should contain four pairs of cards for each child playing. All the letters should be different, eg for five players there should be 20 different letter cards and the matching pictures.

To play, deal four picture cards and four letter cards to each player. The players look at their cards but keep them hidden from the other players. The first player asks any player for the sound (letter) to match a picture card in his hand. She must give the card if she has it. If the first player receives the card he asked for he puts the pair on the table in front of him. Whether a pair has been made or not, play then moves round the table to the next player, who asks for a card in his turn. The winner is the first player to pair all his picture cards with letters.

Look and say words

Objectives

To teach sight recognition of words which cannot easily be built phonically. All children, but particularly those whose visual perception and recall need strengthening, should be taught to look carefully at these words noticing clues such as the pattern of the word and the starting and finishing letters.

Level of development

These words should be taught as soon as children show interest in them when they begin to try to read their own books and come across words such as 'they', 'here' and 'said' which cannot be built phonically at that stage.

Classroom organisation

- Build up a classroom flashcard pack of cards 10cm × 25cm showing the words requested by the children. Flick through it every day as quickly as the children can read the words.

- Use the context of a word to help recall. List clue sentences at the back of a child's work book, with the 'look and say' word picked out with a felt-tip marker.
- Look at the place of the tall letters and tails in a word, then draw a frame round the word to emphasise the pattern. Show the outline of two words and get the children to say which word belongs to each pattern.
- Let children finger-trace a written word saying it as they do so, to strengthen recollection of the letter pattern of a word.
- For children with a better auditory than visual memory convert the visual picture of the word into sound, giving the letters by name, h-e-r-e here.
- Make a matching game as shown on page 106 for children to fit words into their outline.

Visual perception

Objectives

To consolidate the learning of sound/sight links and 'look and say' words by regular daily recall, using flash cards.

To provide activities to strengthen visual perception for children who find flash cards difficult.

Level of development

Flash cards can be used from the start in the teaching of sound/sight links and 'look and say' words. Some children will be able to retain visual impressions easily, others will need additional activities to strengthen their visual perception, before they are able to make good use of flash cards. Easy recall of a letter shape or a word is linked to the clarity with which the letter or letters is perceived in the first place.

Classroom organisation

A number of activities is listed below. Wherever possible, try to relate these to children's interest, especially their reading, and be prepared to adapt them to your classroom projects.

To strengthen visual perception:

- Draw a large figure or letter on the playground. The children walk over the

Walking over the shape of a letter drawn on the playground will help to strengthen the child's visual perception.

shape until they have it clearly in their minds, then walk the shape again without the letter or figure as a guide.
- Sort leaves by their shape, or play any other game calling for sorting by shape not size. Letters should be all sizes. Collect together a tray of items for sorting which are round, square, triangular and so on.
- Have two sets of matching pictures. Spread one set out on a table, show one picture briefly from the other set, then get a child to remember the picture and find the matching one.
- Play Kim's game. Look at a tray of objects for one minute. Recall what was on the tray after it has been taken away. Two useful variations are to bring the tray back with one item missing or one item added which has to be identified.
- Teach a child to take a mental 'photograph' of a shape or letter. Show a flash card of a shape or letter. Let the child look at it intently then shut his eyes and visualise it on the inside of his eyelids. Then he looks straight at his work book and writes the shape. Increase the number of shapes or letters as the child becomes more expert. Some children who find copying difficult will need a lot of this type of exercise.
- Spot the difference in two almost identical pictures cut from comics or magazines.

Using flash cards

- Make separate flash card packs for sounds and for words as soon as any written sounds or 'look and say' words are introduced. A suitable size is 10cm × 25cm. To begin with each card should have only one letter or word on it written in lower case. The pack will be small at first, and to keep an atmosphere of confidence and pride in achievement it should be built up gradually so that the majority of the class can read the whole pack all the time. Flick through the pack regularly every day as quickly as the children can read the cards.
- Use sound flash cards to build words or word flash cards to build sentences to keep the purpose of learning sounds and

words constantly in view. Give three children the letters 'i', 'p' and 'n' to hold up for the class to see. Get a fourth child to arrange them to say 'pin' and another child to make the word 'nip'. Words such as 'here', 'is' and 'Tom' can be arranged in three different ways to make sentences.

- Have flash cards on display in the classroom all day, getting children to place sound cards by objects starting with that sound, or word cards in sentences in relevant places.
- Play 'Simon says' using flash cards giving instructions such as 'stand up', 'jump' etc.
- Make a personal 'look and say' pack of flash cards for slower readers.

Follow-up

Capital letters

Introduce capital letters as they occur. Children's names are a good introduction to capitals. Many children will have been taught to name capital letters before starting school, and will need to learn that 'A' and 'a' both say /ă/.

Put capital letters on the reverse side of the lower case letter flash cards and turn different cards to the capital side each day.

Put words with capital starting letters on the reverse side of word flash cards so that the cards can be turned to give a capital starting letter to a sentence when the cards are used for sentence building.

Visual word building

Objectives

To teach children to read phonic words as soon as possible, to give purpose to the learning of abstract sounds and symbols, and to give them a tool with which they can tackle reading of their choice.

To present word building in a variety of ways to enable each child to find the way that suits him best.

Level of development

The reading of simple two and three letter phonic words should follow from aural word building as soon as enough sound/ sight links to make a few words can be recognised.

Classroom organisation

- Write simple three letter words on the blackboard, using sound/sight links already learned, and practise running the sounds together as in aural word building.
- Write a three letter word on a card and show it to the children, then cut it up into three letters and get them to reassemble it.

In the 'Long card game' a player can re-arrange the pieces on her card to make a space for the ending in her hand.

- Practise combining the first consonant and vowel together, eg 'c' and 'a' to make /că/, then add endings such as 'p', 't' or 'n' to /că/. Write some simple three letter phonic words on card, about 15cm × 7cm and cut off the last letter. Deal one card to each child and let him find a partner who has the other half of his word.
- Combine a vowel and a consonant together, eg 'a' and 't' to make /ăt/, then add starting letters such as 'c', 'h' or 'm'.

  Play the following **Skyscraper game**. Divide the class into four teams, each team to find words ending with different vowel consonant combinations, eg '-an', '-it', '-at', '-ad'. Choose four leaders to write the words on a board or sheet of

paper. Turn up sound flash cards one by one as possible starting letters. If the team can give a word the leader writes it on the board, each team trying to build the highest skyscraper.

- Give practice with vowel sounds. Some children have a lot of difficulty with this, muddling /ă/ and /ŭ/, and /ĭ/ and /ĕ/. Make picture cards of simple three letter words and get the children to sort them into boxes marked /ă/, /ĕ/, /ĭ/, /ŏ/ and /ŭ/ according to the vowel sound in the word.
- Make a card with a movable strip of vowels in the centre, to give practice with short vowels. List the beginning and end letters of six words evenly spaced on a card leaving room in the middle for the movable strip. Make the movable strip twice the height of the card and space 12 vowels evenly on it to match the spacing on the card. Cut a slit to take the strip at the top and the bottom of the card and thread the strip through. Let the children find as many words as they can by moving the strip. Useful word beginnings and endings would be: 'h-m', 'b-d', 't-p', 'h-t', 'd-g' and 'p-n'.

Follow-up

- Play a word building game, the **Long card game** (see page 198). This is a game for two, three or four players. The object of

Sound blending wheels can be used to reinforce consonant blends.

the game is for each player to complete all the words on his card. To play, each player takes a long card and the word ending pieces are put face downwards on the table. Each player in turn picks up one word ending piece and tries to put it on his card where it will make a word, saying the word as he does so. If necessary the pieces on his card may be rearranged to make a space for the ending in his hand. If he cannot use the piece he puts it back, face downwards, on the table. The winner is the first player to complete his card.

To make the game more lively, it could be played with the playing pieces face upwards on the table, and a die together with a chart (see page 199) saying which piece should be picked up.

- Introduce the double sounds 'th', 'sh' and 'ch'. Add them to the flash card pack, and personal phonic packs, and use them for word building.
- Introduce consonant blends such as 'sp', or 'tr', 'bl' and 'st' coming at the beginning of words, aurally and with a consonant-blend flash card pack. Follow this with blends such as 'ng', 'st', 'sp' and 'mp', 'nd' and 'nk' found at the end of words. For practice with these blends using a sound blending wheel (see page 200).

Double sounds and letters which change sounds

Objectives

To carry phonic teaching forward by introducing the idea of two letters combining or reacting on each other to produce a sound other than their two blended sounds, eg two vowels giving a long vowel sound, the 'r' combination sounds such as 'ar', 'or' and 'er', 'c' and 'g' becoming soft before 'e', 'i' and 'y', and the vowel digraphs such as 'oo', 'oi' and 'ou'.

Level of development

These double sounds and changed sounds must be introduced slowly as an on-going part of the build-up of the flash card pack or the personal phonic pack. Some of the first sounds learned can probably be left out of the pack now to keep it a reasonable size, but letters with alternative pronunciations such as the vowels and 'c' and 'g' must be kept in. Each new sound/sight link presented must be well consolidated before a new sound is presented.

Classroom organisation

- Introduce and put into the flash card pack: *'ar'*, *'or'*, and *'er'* with the clue words *'arch'*, *'orchard'* and *'butter'*. ('ir', 'ur' and 'ear' saying /er/ are left until later). Use single sound flash cards to try to find words containing the 'ar' sound, as in the Skyscraper game (see page 110), eg bar, car, far, hard and so on.

- Make a pack of about 30 words using these three digraphs to play **Noughts and crosses** (see page 201 for board and counters.) One player takes the nought counters and the other player takes the crosses. The object of the game is to make a straight line of three crosses or three noughts going horizontally, vertically or diagonally across the board.

    To play, the word cards are shuffled and one card is put face downwards in each square on the board. The rest of the pack is left on one side face downwards. Before a player can place his counter, he must turn up the word on his chosen square and read it aloud. If the other player agrees that it is correct, the first player takes the word card off the board and puts his counter on the square. If the word is not read correctly, the two players work out together what it says before it is replaced face downwards on the square. In this case, the player misses that turn, but should remember the word next time round. Play continues with the players taking alternate turns until one player has completed a line of three.

    Each time a line is 'won', remove the counters from the board, and cover the empty squares again from the pack, for another round of the game. The game ends when there are insufficient cards left in the pack to cover all nine of the squares on the board. The winner is the player who has won the greater number of games.

- The long vowel or lazy 'e' rule. Teach by adding an 'e' to the end of a short vowel word, eg 'hat' becoming 'hate', and add the vowel sound to the relevant flash card, ie the 'a' card will now be read /ă/ and /ā/ and the 'o' card as /ŏ/, and /ō/. Teach the rule, 'a long vowel needs another vowel near' at this stage. It will help later in the reading of syllable words.

    Another useful rule to teach at this stage is that two vowels can 'hold hands' over one consonant (and affect the first vowel), but they cannot reach to hold hands over two or more consonants (eg ape, apple).

    Use the **Noughts and crosses** game (page 201) (see previous instructions) for practice in reading long and short vowels.

- Continue the idea of one letter affecting another with 'e', and 'i' and 'y' making 'c' and 'g' soft. 'c' before 'e', 'i' and 'y' says /s/, eg I *cy*cle to the *ce*ntre of the *ci*ty. A flash card pack with 'ca', 'ce', 'ci', 'co' and 'cu', 'cy' and 'ch' could be used to practise quick recognition of 'c's different sounds.

    Another rule to grapple with at this stage is that 'g' is always soft (saying /j/) in the middle of words before 'e', 'i' and 'y', and at the end of a word before 'e'. When 'g' is at the beginning of a word before 'e', 'i' or 'y' pupils must learn to try both the /g/ and /j/ sounds.

    Mnemonic sentence: The *Ge*rman at the *gym*khana had *gi*nger hair.

    Whenever possible look for examples of these rules in sentences taken from 'real life'. Listen to the children's own speech and look in their reading books for uses of these rules. The more they see them used, the more they will come to recognise them and will be able to use them when looking for contextual clues.

- **Lotto** (see page 202) can be used to give practice in reading words spelled with a soft 'c'. It can be played with two, three or four players. One player is chosen as caller and has the pack of caller's cards face downwards on the table in front of him. The other players each take a lotto card.

    To start play the caller reads the top card from his pack. If a player has this word on his lotto card he calls 'yes' and puts his finger on the word. The caller checks that it is the same as the word he is holding, then gives the card to the player to cover the word on his board. If two players both claim the same word it is given to the first one to call. If a player fails to recognise the word, it should be pointed out to him before the word card is put back into the caller's pack. The winner is the first player to complete his board. The game can be repeated, giving each player a turn at being caller.

When playing with just two players, each player should have their own lotto card. The players take it in turns to read a card for the other to identify on his own board. The caller may not claim the card for himself. If it is not claimed it should be put back into the middle of the pack.

- Look at two vowels together, 'ai', 'ee' or 'ea', 'oa' and 'ue', recall that a long vowel needs another vowel near and teach the rhyme:
'When two vowels go out walking
The first one does the talking'.
Notice the different spelling of the long vowel sounds at the beginning or middle and at the end of a word, and the awkward 'igh' for /ī/ in single syllable words.

	Word beginning or middle	Word ending
/ā/	ai	ay
/ē/	ee, ea	ee
/ō/	oa	ow
/ī/	igh	y
/ū/	oo	ew, ue

- The **Switch** game (see page 203) will give practice in reading long vowel sounds in the middle of words.

To start play, shuffle the cards and deal seven cards to each player. The players look at their cards, and the rest of the pack is put face downwards on the table. The first player puts one of his cards face upwards on the table, saying the spelling at the top of the card and reading the word, eg 'a, i, rain'. The next player must play a card containing the same long vowel sound, placing it on top of the card already played and giving the spelling and the word as he does so. Alternatively, if he cannot follow with the same vowel sound, or if he wants to change the vowel sound for his next turn, he may play a word *starting with the same letter* as the one on the table and say 'Switch to . . .' giving the spelling he is switching to, and reading out his new word. If a player cannot play a matching vowel or a matching starting letter, he must draw a card from the main pack, and, if it is suitable, he may play it on that turn. The winner is the player who gets rid of all his cards first, or is left with the lowest number of cards when no more can be played.

- Children with poor visual recall will need to learn all double sounds (digraphs) with a clue word and to practise them in their personal phonic pack. For example the vowel digraphs 'oi' – oil, 'oy' – boy, 'ou' – out, 'ow' – cow, 'au' – autumn, 'aw' – jaws

Older children will enjoy the element of competition in games such as 'Switch'.

and the new 'r' digraphs 'ir' – sir, 'ur' – urgent, 'ear' – earth.

- Play **Road sense** for reading practice with these double sounds (see page 204), for two, three or four players. A die is required for this game. The object of the game is for each player to go from his home to the roundabout, then leaving the roundabout by a different exit, to go home by a different route. Road signs must be observed.

   To play, the word pack is shuffled and placed face downwards on the table and each player takes a counter and puts it on his home square. The first player throws the die. The number on the die tells him the number of cards he must pick up from the card pack and read out loud. He may make one move forward for each word he reads correctly. When a card has been read it is put on a discard pile face upwards. Play continues in this way until the players get back to their

By making a new set of cards, the 'Road sense board' can be used to reinforce any phonic skill being taught.

homes. When the word card pack is used up the discard pack is shuffled, turned face downwards and used again as the word pack.

Syllable words

Objectives

To enable children to read most English words by using phonics and phonic rules in the reading of multi-syllable words. Reading words of more than one syllable presents two problems, firstly where to divide the syllables, and secondly where to put the stress in the word. In addition children will need to be familiar with the more complex spellings such as 'tion', 'sion', 'le' and 'ture' found at the ends of words.

Level of development

The building of two syllable words where each syllable has a short vowel, eg intend, trumpet, happen and puppet, or a familiar digraph such as 'ar', eg garden, market and carpet can be started as soon as building simple three and four letter words has been mastered.

The concept of vowels being long or short will have to be grasped before words where the first vowel is long, such as over, basin and crazy can be read phonically.

Classroom organisation

- A helpful, though by no means watertight rule to teach for syllable division is: Divide into syllables between two consonants or in front of one consonant.

When the syllables are divided in this way, if a syllable ends in a vowel that vowel will usually be long, eg spi/der.

Where a syllable ends in a consonant, the vowel will usually be short, because using the syllable division rule there will be two consonants before the next vowel. This vowel will be too far away to lengthen the first vowel eg den/tist. Reinforce the concept of syllables with long or short vowels with the **Syllable sums** game (for two, three or four players). The cards (see page 206) are sorted into two packs, word starters and word endings. Four word starters are dealt to each player, then both packs are placed face downwards on the table.

To play, the first player takes a word ending and tries to use it to make a word with one of his word starters. If he is unable to use it he puts it face upwards on a throw-away pile. If he makes a word he replaces the word starter he has used with a new word starter from the pack. The next player may take the discarded card from the top of the throw-away pile or an unseen card from the word ending pack. When the word ending pack is used up, the throw-away pile is turned over and re-used until no more cards are left. The winner is the player with the greatest number of completed words on the table.

- Look for the stress in nursery rhymes, and say them emphasising the stress, eg *Jack* and *Jill* went *up* the hill, to *fetch* a *pail* of *water*.

Try changing the stress: Jack *and* Jill, or Jack and *Jill*. Look at the stress in words such as 'answer' and 'reply'. Most English words have the stress on the first syllable unless there is a prefix. Finding the stress in words will need a lot of practice, but once the idea is mastered children will be able to look at a new word and try putting the stress in different places, until they find a word that they recognise.

Play the **Stress guessing game**. Make a list on the blackboard of six words with the stress on the first syllable, eg awful, typist, litter, visit, blossom and cancel, then a list of words with the stress on the second syllable, eg rely, annoy, delay, avoid, forget and control. Each player in turn claps a word then says it and a word from the other list. His opponents have to listen and identify which word was clapped.

Teach 'tion' and 'ssion' saying /shŭn/. When necessary, add this to the flash card and personal phonic packs. 'sion' usually says /zyŭn/ as in 'television'. This is a useful spelling rule, but need not be taught as a separate phonic sound for reading. In words ending 'tion', 'ssion' and 'sion' the stress is always on the vowel preceding these endings, eg dictátion, posséssion, and divísion. Practise saying words with these endings emphasising the stress.

Get the children to listen to words such as 'connect', 'depress', 'devote', and 'infect', then to repeat them back with a /shŭn/ ending, eg connection, depression and so on.

- Teach other complex endings 'ture' /cher/, 'our' /er/, 'ous' /ŭs/, and 'le' as they occur, adding them to flash card and personal phonic packs where necessary. Make a **Happy families** game using 12 different word-ending families to give practice in these more complex endings.

The families should be groups of

115

words with similar endings. Each card should have one of the four words written across the middle of the card, with the word family at the top and other words in the family listed at the bottom. A player may ask any other player for a card by name, if he has one card of that family in his hand. If he gets the card he asks for, he has another turn. If not, the turn passes to the player who failed to supply the requested card.

Suggested word families:

-ation	-ible
sensation	horrible
dictation	terrible
relation	legible
preparation	accessible

-sion (/zyŭn/)	-able
television	reliable
division	noticeable
erosion	advisable
evasion	conceivable

-ssion	-ought
confession	bought
passion	nought
permission	thought
agression	fought

-our	-ary
colour	temporary
flavour	tributary
humour	voluntary
harbour	secretary

-ture	-ous
nature	curious
future	continuous
creature	previous
puncture	fabulous

-gue	-ance
league	appearance
tongue	resistance
rogue	ignorance
plague	guidance

Strategies for reluctant readers

Objectives

To motivate reluctant readers to take a renewed interest in learning reading skills by defining the areas where they need special help and by harnessing their own interests. They may be trying to read material which is too difficult for them or lacking in interest, or there may be gaps in their learning of phonics which have been overlooked.

Level of development

Children may begin to lose interest in reading at any stage, and a teacher needs constantly to be aware of their varying needs and abilities. Always be ready to adopt a fresh approach or deal with any particular difficulties a child is having bearing in mind all the time that reading should be a pleasant and rewarding experience.

Classroom organisation

• Find a source of motivation by seeking out a child's particular interests and reading with him about these. Help him to appreciate the *usefulness* of reading: read signs such as names of shops, pubs, bus routes, current films and so on; read instructions for construction kits, names of football teams and football results in the newspaper.

• Build a reader's confidence by presenting her with plenty of reading material which is well within her capacity. Give her encouragement at every opportunity and don't overlook *any* source of reading that interests her: comics, quiz books, jokes etc.

• Avoid embarrassing her by asking her to read aloud in front of the class.

• Get the children to prepare a 'reading' tape. Record them reading a page or a paragraph. Look again at the piece together, reviewing difficult words, phrasing and so on. Ask the children to re-read the piece playing the tape with the sound turned down low. The child can then compare against his previous best.

• The chapters on 'The apprenticeship approach' and 'The shared reading approach' contain further ideas for helping children to use contextual clues.

Let the children write, illustrate and read their own stories.

Resources

Alpha to Omega (3rd Edition) Bev Hornsby and Frula Shear, Heinemann Educational Books Limited (1980)

The Pictogram System Lynn Wendon, Pictogram Supplies, Barton, Cambridge CB3 7AY

Games to Exercise Your Spelling Elizabeth Wood, E J Arnold and Son Limited

More Games to Exercise Your Spelling Elizabeth Wood, E J Arnold and Son Limited

Exercise Your Spelling, Books 1, 2 and 3 Elizabeth Wood, Edward Arnold (Publishers) Ltd

Advanced reading skills

Advanced reading skills

INTRODUCTION

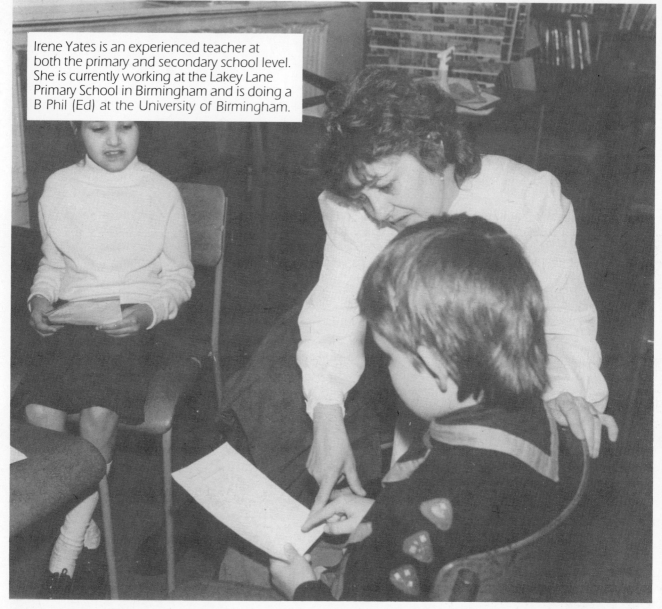

Irene Yates is an experienced teacher at both the primary and secondary school level. She is currently working at the Lakey Lane Primary School in Birmingham and is doing a B Phil (Ed) at the University of Birmingham.

What is meant by advanced reading skills? Essentially, they are all the different skills which a child needs to acquire in addition to simple decoding in order to gain meaning. Thus sequencing and scanning techniques come under this heading as does the development of dictionary and index skills. Often it is assumed that these skills will come of their own accord, just by the pupil reading. For some children they do, but for some they most definitely do not.

Take a piece of legal text for example. You will probably be able to verbalise it quite competently even to the point of good expression, but few adults without a law degree would be able to fully comprehend its meaning.

Compare this with some of the

'competent' readers in your school. They talk away – perfectly able so far as fluency, and even expression, is concerned – but do they understand what they are reading? Much of this problem is, of course, to do with *their* concept of reading, not ours. *We* know that reading isn't just a question of relating the symbols to sounds, learning the 'tricks' of intonation, juggling with the phonics and jumping through the hoops of various reading schemes. But do *they*? If it's not getting inside their heads, being re-organised and stimulating reflection then it's not *reading*!

It is a commonly accepted belief that some children learn to manipulate numbers, find patterns in them, and make them function in their daily lives, whilst others learn only to follow the rules and 'do sums'. Perhaps the same instinctive responses apply to readers. To some children, reading is a challenging part of normal living, to others it remains a mystery for years (or worse, forever!). It is something they 'do' in a decoding sense, which has no function in their lives. This is not to say that advanced reading skills are 'cures'; however their development does go some way towards providing children with the keys to unlock some of the mystique they find themselves immersed in.

Advanced reading skills are in themselves something of an enigma, for as soon as a child can actually decode, she has to begin to employ advanced skills in order to read.

In our current education system, the child who has learned to read will progress to being a child who must read to learn. Whether you agree with the 'textbook' approach or not, it's here to stay at the moment, particularly at the secondary level. You can't help but sympathise with the child who functions at the level of simple decoding as she struggles against an inability to reflect, re-organise and reshape.

By giving a child time to learn and practise study skills, you are giving her a tool she can refine throughout her life. The time spent on developing those skills in primary school is time that can never be other than well spent.

If you feel complacent about the fluent, competent readers in your class ask yourself a few basic questions: Do the constraints of your classroom make it inevitable that you focus on fluency and expression to the detriment of the kind of interpretation that leads to cognitive and personal development? Are your teaching strategies for advanced reading skills clear enough? Do you allow (or even encourage) your pupils to become passive readers, asking little of texts and/or authors? Are your pupils actually stretched by/involved in the texts that they read? Do you provide a purpose for reading? Do you allow your children sufficient time to immerse themselves in their reading?

Providing opportunities

Of course, no amount of skills training in the world will turn children into readers if they are not given the opportunity! Children should be encouraged to make their own selections from a constant and steadily changing supply of books that is easily accessible.

Apart from access to books, what children need more than anything else for developing advanced reading skills, is *time*: time to read, time to think and time to talk. *Talking about reading* is as essential an activity as reading itself. Apart from anything else, it is during discussion that the teacher can pass on her enthusiasm. Although at first glance discussion sometimes appears to be just a 'waste of time' when there is so much on the curriculum, children pick up a great deal from their teacher's attitudes.

Progress in the development of advanced reading skills can be monitored with a simple checklist. Reading achievement of course is different for each individual and it's up to the teacher to discover what kind of help each pupil needs.

The goal of each teacher should be to ensure that each child in the class will eventually experience the thrill of achievement and the satisfaction of leaving the swings and roundabouts of controlled vocabulary to read with complete understanding, purely for the love of it.

Sequencing

Objectives

In order to understand what's going on in a text the reader needs to be able to retain what he has already read in his mind whilst anticipating what is to come next – the process is a kind of cognitive balance between what's behind and what's ahead; there is a need to disassemble the material and put it back together logically. Giving children the chance to manipulate texts will help them to develop this skill.

Level of development

As long as the child has the ability to break down and restructure with concrete materials, the material used for this task will depend upon the reading level of the individual child. It can be accomplished with very simple material, leading on to more complex texts with more competent readers.

Classroom organisation

Children learn by doing, and the best way to teach sequencing is to provide them with opportunities to do it themselves. Write out or photocopy several pieces of text. These could be poems, comic strips, photo-strip stories and (for really good readers) chapters of novels. Cut them into small chunks (eg two or three lines for poems) and place each one in an envelope. (It helps to give a clue on the envelope so that they know what they're looking for). Let the children work in pairs or groups to put the text back together so that it makes sense. Encourage them to discuss what they are doing and to read aloud to each other as they go along. Make sure that they are looking for clues all the time which tell them the right order. If you have a computer with a word processing facility it can be used for sequencing activities, moving chunks of text in exactly the same way as they would when physically moving bits of paper about.

Young children can practise sequencing using a series of cards showing an activity that has a sequential pattern. As with the chunks of text, jumble them up and ask the child to put them into the correct order. Older children might enjoy sequencing a set of (undated) correspondence.

To make the task more abstract have the children record into a tape recorder as they are sequencing. When they get to the end they can listen to their tape to find out if they've made any mistakes. Alternatively, read a story to the children, then ask them to tell it as they remember it on to a tape. Let them play it back to a friend who can challenge the sequence if it's wrong.

Sequencing activities need not always be text related. Ask the children to determine the route taken in a railway/air journey. Give them names of towns/cities between a point of departure and a point of arrival and ask them to determine the route taken using maps and atlases.

Follow-up

Once they have the idea of sequencing events and ideas, let the children make up their own stories, draw their own cards etc to challenge their friends. Though it sounds simple, this is quite difficult and they will often leave out several stages. The fact that their friends can challenge them will show them the importance of sequencing.

This kind of activity lends itself very well to theme work and to books that you are reading to the class. You can ask them to make synopses of fiction they have read for others in the class to sequence.

When they have mastered this they can have lots of fun structuring their own story plots. Remember – they only have to write short synopses, not the narrative!

Each line of a poem will have to be read carefully to determine the correct order.

Skimming and scanning

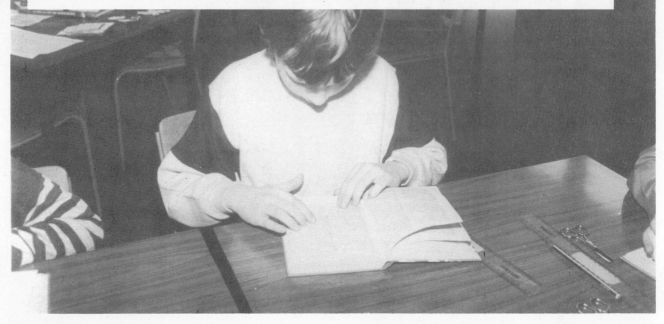

Objectives

Once the child can read fairly fluently she should be encouraged to develop techniques for reading at different speeds. For instance, the speed at which she should read when trying to find a number in the telephone directory should be faster than when she is savouring a chapter in a book being read for pleasure. An ideal way to practise skimming and scanning techniques is to work with the class through the stages that they should go through in selecting a book for topic work. The following strategy can be applied to develop 'selection' rather than random choice.

Level of development

Skimming and scanning techniques can be used with children of all reading abilities, provided you monitor the level of the reference books you are providing. If they are too complex an early reader may be put off. On the other hand, competent fluent readers need challenging material. Work in small groups at first and take them clearly through the steps.

Classroom organisation

Have a specific topic subject firmly in mind. Ask the children to start their scanning by looking at the front and back covers, then the contents page and index to get an idea of the subject covered. Ask them to glance through the pages at headings and sub-headings and to read through the introduction or preface to get an idea of the level of the book. If the book is not what they need, or is too simple or too difficult, encourage them to abandon it and start again.

Once they have found a book ask them to read through some sections of the text rapidly to grasp its main subject and level of readability. Reading the beginning and ending of a paragraph will often tell the child what it's about. Impress upon the class that it is a good idea to skim a chapter two or three times to gain a general impression of it before beginning detailed reading.

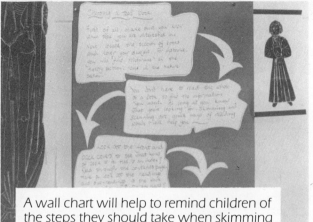

A wall chart will help to remind children of the steps they should take when skimming and scanning.

SQ3R

'SQ3R' is a simple strategy to teach children which will assist them in independent study. It helps to stop them from 'copying out of books', which is what they often do when doing 'topic' work.

SQ3R means, very simply: Survey, Question, Read, Review and Record

- Survey means use skimming and scanning techniques to get a general picture of the information in the text and to locate specific information. The children should be shown how to make simple notes of information they wish to retain, notes which they may expand on later when writing in full.
- Question means apply the six formula questions to the text: how? who? what? when? where? why? Test their relevance and seek their answers.
- Read, review, record means read for information, organise information gleaned into own words, and record in graphic and written form.

Follow-up

As with every aspect of reading skills, constant practice is essential. Use atlases, telephone directories, business directories, etc to practise scanning techniques. By preparing workcards in advance eg 'What's the name of the person on page 176 whose number is 123?' to go with a particular directory you will be able to provide hours of useful research skill development.

Examples of work-cards to develop index skills

When designing cards it is essential to remain aware of the objective, that is to develop research skills. All too often the *information itself* becomes the important focus of topic work.

It means a slight difference in approach, as shown in the following two workcards. In the first card the *information* that is to be gathered is the crucial part of the exercise, whilst in the second card the important activity is actually *locating* the information.

Workcard 1

Using the *Mind Alive Encyclopedia of the World*, turn to the section on Asia which you will find by using the contents list at the front of the book. Find out:

- How much of the earth's land surface is covered by the USSR.
- The name of the second largest mountain lake in the world.
- The normal temperature of the Omyakon Plateau in Siberia.

Workcard 2

In one of the books on this table you can find out a great deal of information about the USSR, including how much land surface it covers, the name of the second largest mountain lake in the world, the name of the largest plateau in Siberia and its normal everyday temperature.

- Examine the books and decide which you will need to use.
- USSR is an abbreviation for which country? You will need to know which continent it is in; find out from an atlas or dictionary.
- Use both the contents page and the index to locate the information you require.
- On a card, note the information you have gathered, together with any other interesting facts and show exactly where the information can be checked.

127

Dictionary skills

Objectives

All teachers will be familiar with children asking 'Please Miss, how do I spell . . .?' Familiarisation with dictionaries will go a long way towards alleviating this. Encourage children to use scanning techniques and to read at speed when using dictionaries, putting what they have learned to good use. Reinforcement of alphabetical order is essential. Only then will they really begin to learn to use a dictionary for their own purposes.

A 'zigzag alphabet' will help to reinforce alphabetical order.

Level of development

Any child who has any success in decoding, and who can recognise initial letters should be taught to use a dictionary. Try to match the dictionaries used to some degree with the child's ability. For instance, a reluctant reader might find a picture dictionary more helpful than one with thousands of words and small print.

Classroom organisation

Take the time to examine the structure of dictionaries and books in general, with the children. Get them to study the copyright pages. Discuss the role of the publisher, the printer, the ISBN, the compiler and the copyright mark, in the production of the book. Once they have learned the difference between authors, compilers, publishers, etc let them explore the school library with the aim of finding books published by the same house, or printed by the same printer. Ask open-ended questions such as, 'Does every book carry a © mark somewhere?' 'Can you find several books written by the same author?' 'Is the same publisher involved each time?' This will help them to explore and 'get the feel' of reference books. The more they can talk with their peers the better.

Using the contents page

Although the contents page will tell the children exactly where each letter section of the dictionary is, this fact is not always apparent to them. Spend plenty of time looking at the sections. Ask them to estimate the biggest section, the smallest section etc. You could ask them to estimate the number of words in a particular section and then challenge their friends to estimate or guess. Try to turn your activities into 'games'. The children will enjoy them much more that way.

Spot the word

Spot the word is a wonderful game to play as a whole class, but it does mean that each child, or at least each pair, should have the same dictionary. Pick a word and say 'Find the word that begins with . . . and means . . . .' Give plenty of time so that everyone in the class can find the word. Half-way through the game point out the words at the top of the columns and ask them to find the relationship between them and the words on the page. When they become really fast at finding words, let them play in small

groups. Although this is a simple game, it is very enjoyable. Because the length of time can be varied it is a productive way of using up any odd spare minutes.

Word rockets

Alphabetical order is an incredibly difficult concept for some children. Although they understand the sequence of the alphabet and they know what initial letters are, second and third letter alphabetical sequence tends to be a complete blur! Having the children make word rockets will help to sort these problems out as well as give some basic concepts of linguistics. Each child should cut out her rocket shape from coloured card. She then chooses a word – for example 'apple', which she writes on to card, cuts out and places on the rocket shape. She then has to find a word in the dictionary that begins with the last two letters of 'apple', eg 'length' which she adds to the shape in a similar manner. The game continues in this way until the rocket is full. It is possible to vary the game by using a different shape – one which fits in with your topic theme perhaps, and by sticking to words which are useful to that theme.

Progress to using the last three letters instead of two. This is extremely challenging. As a follow-up activity children could be asked to pick a string of half a dozen words and weave them into a story. Some of the stories will be very interesting!

Children will have to refer frequently to their dictionaries when making word rockets.

Follow-up

'My aunty likes' is another fun game to play. Start by saying 'My aunty likes puppies but she doesn't like cats. My aunty likes umbrellas but she doesn't like rain. My aunty likes coffee but she doesn't like tea' – the secret being that 'my aunty' only likes words which have a double letter in them. Children have to find out the rule, and are not allowed to suggest what it is, only to give examples. Let them know if they're right. If they aren't let them know which of their words is correct, eg 'She likes feet but not toes', or if both are wrong 'She doesn't like either of those'. Eventually most children will be so puzzled they will have to use a dictionary to look at the words. The bright ones who catch on must not give away the secret but use their dictionaries to glean more examples.

Index skills

Objectives

Encourage your children to develop a methodical approach to the selection of reference books for work on a topic. So often teachers say 'Go and find a book about . . .' without giving the children any strategies for making their choice, which can then only be haphazard. Once they have learned to apply study techniques they will use them all the time.

Level of development

Children are ready for this activity when they have thoroughly accommodated dictionary skills.

Classroom organisation

Topic work is an ideal time to develop index skills. By researching beforehand, you will be able to pose questions which you know they will be able to find solutions to if they make the right selection. This entails thorough preparation on your part.

However, to begin with, it is possible to teach the use of indexes with a fairly random selection of material. Provide a collection of reference books and allow the children to choose their own subjects for study. Encourage them to use their skimming and scanning techniques when making their selection. The next step is for them to look down the index for the subject they are researching. If they cannot find it, encourage them to think of an alternative word.

On finding the subject, they should make a note of the name of the book, the page and/or illustration numbers. Scan the page to see if they have the required information.

If the book does not have the information the child needs, the child should abandon it and start again – and *not give up*!

Using the contents page

Some children will find using the contents page a far simpler method than using the index, but they should be encouraged to use both. The child should read the contents page carefully, then turn to the beginning of the chapter that seems to have the required information. If the chapter has sub-headings they should be used for pinpointing the information being sought. If there are no sub-headings the only way is to skim beginnings and ends of paragraphs for main idea.

If the information is there, the child should make a note of the book, the page etc. If not, the book should be abandoned and another selected.

Making inferences

Objectives

Children should be taught to go beyond the obvious, to examine the implications of what they have read and to make

deductions using their own perceptions. Children are naturally curious, but often seem to have lost the habit of thinking for themselves. They need to be encouraged to read between the lines.

Level of development

Since what you are asking the child to do in this kind of exercise is to *think* and *frame questions*, it can be done at any level. With non-readers the use of pictures and posters is crucial, so that they will develop inference skills before they actually come to texts.

Comprehension at inferential level is far more developed than comprehension at literal level. The child should be able to understand the way the text is moving at the stated level before being asked to make any logical, pragmatic or deductive inferences.

Encourage children to make inferences about all the texts they read.

Classroom organisation

For any age group posters are a useful discussion point for developing inference skills. Start by talking with the children about what you can see. Encourage them to look for minute details! Move on to what you can't see – ask questions beginning with 'why', 'how', 'who', 'where' and 'when'. Let the class weave a whole story around the picture, beginning at a point before the picture was 'taken' and then go on to 'What's going to happen next?'.

Questions, written either by yourself or the children could be taped up by the poster. Make card and sticky tape readily available so that they can put up a question when they think of it. In all cases it is essential to recognise and discuss all the obvious, *literal* details before the children can begin to go beyond.

Follow-up

Tell the class the beginning of a story, then divide the children into groups and let each group hypothesise how they think the story will end. Each group should then be encouraged to present their ending to the rest of the class.

Making books

Once the children are used to formulating questions, they could move on to making books or folders using magazine, retail catalogues and travel brochures etc. Working on their own (or in pairs if it helps them to formulate questions), they can choose pictures and using their existing knowledge, predict possible situations and eventualities. The emphasis should be upon seeing beyond what the picture tells them.

Anticipation

There is no more effective way to help children hypothesise about a text than for them to talk about it. It does not have to be limited to breaking off mid-sentence and saying 'What's going to happen?' while you are reading to them yourself; it's the kind of pragmatic discussion that should be going on constantly. Children are expected to hypothesise during science lessons, but rarely find the time to talk about what they are reading, what they are watching on TV at home, what kind of sense they are making of the world from newspapers and magazines they read.

An interesting and stimulating way of deciding what comes next is to take a situation from a text, newspaper, television programme or whatever, and, after discussing what has happened so far and the characters of those involved, set them to *act out* what they see as the logical development of the plot. They must, of course, be able to defend their hypothesis by referring to the 'text'.

Critical thinking of this kind will help children to examine their own written work. It will help them to realise how much of what they meant to signify or imply has been missed out! It is only when they begin to realise the huge imaginative leap they have to make in order to infer implied meaning, that they can understand the gaps in their own written or taped stories!

Another possibility is to ask the children to take their favourite book or story and 'cut' it into serial form, ignoring chapter endings, treating it as a 'radio' serial. Each 'programme' should end at a point where the listener wants to know what happens next. Discuss the possibilities at the end of each 'programme'. Perhaps you could tape a few of their ideas.

Modelling

Objectives

Modelling encourages the children to read for meaning and retain information. Before they can translate the text into a visual or written scene they will have had to carefully read and re-read the text and discuss it with others.

Level of development

Monitor the material to suit the level of the child. Use a book or story that you are currently reading to the children, as it is confusing to use text in isolation.

Classroom organisation

Let the children work in pairs or small groups and decide for themselves the kind of representation they want to attempt, eg drawings, cartoon strips, graphs, maps, plans, diagrams etc. They should then skim the text for general impressions and scan for vital information. They will have to think logically and sequentially in order to plan their model and go beyond the literal level of the text in order to perceive an overall picture.

When the model is complete, they

should be able to rationalise it to each other and to the teacher; compare other reconstructions and discuss the advantages and disadvantages of each. They can also present their model to peers who have not read the text and ask them to explain what they see.

Some children may prefer to produce a written representation rather than a visual one. Encourage them to produce a story written in the same style as the one they are exploring. This is called 'stylistic' modelling and uses exactly the same processes as those described previously.

Encouraging an evaluative response

Objectives

Children are notorious for thinking that there are *right* answers and *wrong* answers. They need to be encouraged to share their thoughts to give them confidence in expressing their own considered evaluation.

Level of development

Children of all ages should be encouraged to discuss their opinions, but of course the expectations you have of their response will be different. With any age group their responses will improve with practice. Use the book you are currently reading to the children as it is confusing to use text in isolation.

Classroom organisation

If this is a new type of activity for your children it is best to work in small, friendly groups. Have the children visualise an event or scene. Ask them open ended questions such as: 'How did this situation arise?' 'What do you think will happen next and why?' 'How do you think it will end?'

The children may want to link what has happened in the story with an incident from their own life. You will of course receive many anecdotes but these should be encouraged because they are children's stories and a true and genuine response to what they have absorbed from the text.

Encourage the children to tell what they feel about the character, setting or incident. Equally important is for them to discuss what they feel about the way the author is telling the story. Thematic work lends itself naturally to follow up activities. For example they could act out a scene, write a sequel or illustrate an event in comic book format. More suggestions are given in the chapter on 'Developing a love of books.'

Resources

Finding Information in Non-Fictional Books (A Flowchart for Children) Centre for the Teaching of Reading, School of Education, University of Reading, 29 Eastern Avenue, Reading RG1 6RU

Dictionaries – a list of dictionaries available by Ginny Lapag, Centre for the Teaching of Reading, University of Reading

Junior Education posters by Scholastic Publications Ltd.

Developing a love of books

Developing a love of books

INTRODUCTION

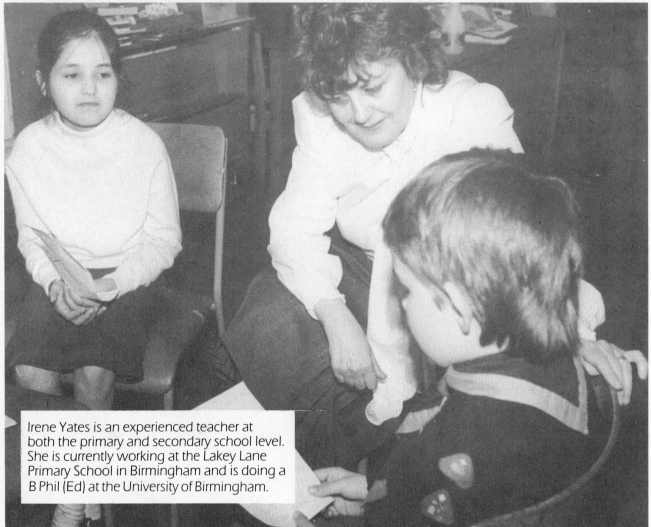

Irene Yates is an experienced teacher at both the primary and secondary school level. She is currently working at the Lakey Lane Primary School in Birmingham and is doing a B Phil (Ed) at the University of Birmingham.

Nobody knows how a child learns to read. There are lots of theories of course, and unlimited strategies, methods and techniques – some of which work for some teachers and some children. But, not *everything* works for *everybody*.

Somehow the magic 'key' that unlocks the mind to literacy defies definition. The only thing that everyone can be certain of is that the motivation to learn to read comes from desire and where that desire is not intrinsic to the child, it has to be induced by others.

It would seem silly to expect a child to develop a desire to learn phonics, or to understand about the complexities of digraphs, dipthongs, synthesis etc.

Yet often this is the way reading is presented in schools. It's not surprising that some children never learn to love books.

Remember how you learned to ride a bike when you were little? Nobody tried to explain to you about the energy required to push the wheels round etc. Instead they said, 'Here's a bike! Get on and ride it!' You probably fell off a few times before you mastered it, but the falling off was important – it showed you where you were going wrong and was part of the challenge. Because you were so determined to be off on your own you kept trying until you managed it. *But you never tried without the bike!* It sounds silly, doesn't it? How could you possibly learn to ride a bike without riding one? Well, how can you possibly learn to read a story, without having a story to read?

Why should learning to read be so different from learning to ride a bike? There is no reason for teachers to make it more difficult than it needs to be. The emphasis should be on fun, pleasure, habit and success, instead of on work, tests, difficulty and failure.

Why are some children avid readers and others reluctant? Evidence shows that children from book-owning homes take more naturally to reading than those from homes where no one reads. Reading makes sense to them from the minute their mother balances them on her lap and points to the pictures in the baby book.

They can see that it has a purpose and a function all of its own. Above all, it's associated with warmth, love and pleasure. The child who comes to school never having handled a book in her life is at a severe disadvantage. She watches other children read, thinks she can't and so doesn't. The child who *can* read, *does* read, and so gets better. The child to whom it seems pointless, lags further and further behind.

Television, the dreaded monster in the corner of the lounge, has become a competitor to reading. Children are attracted to it because it offers such an easy, passive ride. Reading, by comparison, is hard work because it insists upon engaging the mind and the imagination. The hours today's children spend in front of the television are often the hours earlier generations spent reading. Occasionally television is on your side – providing programmes that motivate children to read follow-up books. When it does we should be thankful!

There are problems of course. Not all children live in homes where they can escape from the noise of the family, TV,

visitors, etc. Blithely, teachers nag their pupils to read at home or in bed, never truly knowing the family circumstances that might prevent them from doing so.

It isn't enough to provide pupils with a selection of books and the ability to decode them. Schools must also give them the time and the place in which to learn to love them. It is our responsibility to stimulate good reading habits, and this can be done by trying to foster a love of books.

There are many ways to stimulate and promote enthusiasm for reading. The ideas given in this chapter are not inclusive nor would they work in isolation. It is hoped however, that many or all of them used at different times, consistently and discriminately, will together provide a book-centred nucleus for the classroom and the school.

It is important to give children time during school hours to read for pleasure.

Undirected reading sessions

Objectives

Sustained silent reading sessions will help to establish reading as a pleasurable habit. This kind of activity needs to be well planned, not just left to chance. Often silent reading is something children only do when they have 'finished' their other work. This means that they only ever read in fits and starts unless they read for recreation at home. Like all good habits, silent reading should be started early and established as the normal expectation.

Level of development

Lengthen the time of your silent sustained reading periods according to the needs and development of the children. There is no reason why infants shouldn't be expected to 'read' quietly each day for a while. Those at the picture book stage should get just as much pleasure from the activity as more able readers.

Classroom organisation

Agree a limited amount of time for the activity. Fifteen minutes is a good time to start with. Make it clear that no one is allowed to interrupt anyone, for any reason, during this time. If you choose a particular time each day, say the first 15 minutes of the afternoon, the children will soon get to know what's required and begin to look forward to it. They should not have to make any kind of record of this activity, neither should they be involved in talking to or reading to the teacher.

Ask the children to select their own reading material beforehand and do not allow them to change it during the period of reading. You might allow someone with a very short concentration span to have two or three items of reading material to begin with. Let them choose whatever reading material they prefer. Periodicals, newspapers, magazines, etc should be allowed as well as books. What is important is that the choosing is done before the start of the activity and that they aren't allowed to change it once the session is started. Remember it was their choice.

During the session you should act as a role model and read for pleasure yourself. At the end of the period of time, all reading matter should be put away quickly till next time and the children should get ready for the next activity.

Put a note on the classroom door so that you won't be disturbed. Some teachers like to display a sign saying 'USSR' (standing for Uninterrupted Sustained Silent Reading). If you can get the whole school to join in so much the better (tell the secretary to take the 'phone off the hook!).

Allow children to choose their own reading material.

Reading aloud to children

Objectives

Listening is a very difficult thing to do and teachers learn very quickly that it is impossible to engage all the class's attention at all times! Reading aloud is an ideal way of creating a willingness to listen. It shows children what books are for; it brings them in contact with new authors, new styles of writing, new ideas. When reading aloud to children you can use books they might not otherwise be able to read independently. It helps to show them 'what's in it for them' and gives them an incentive to carry on reading.

Level of development

Storytime or reading aloud is often limited to very young children. Children of all ages, however, will benefit from and enjoy being read to. Choose a book suitable to the age range of your class. It is not essential that they understand all the vocabulary used but they should be able to understand the basic storyline.

Classroom organisation

Reading sessions need to be planned carefully. They are ways of showing children that you feel books are important. By choosing a book at random and not planning how you will read it to the children you are actually saying 'reading doesn't matter – it's not important for me to organise it properly' thus encouraging children to develop negative attitudes towards storybooks.

Choose a book which you enjoyed reading yourself. If you don't, your dislike will probably shine through. Take the time to re-read it again silently. Ask yourself: does the plot move quickly enough to sustain the children's interest? Are the characters clear and well rounded? Does it have some good, crisp dialogue? You may need to condense some of the long, descriptive passages. If you don't feel that the children will want to go back and read it for themselves, perhaps it isn't the right book.

Always have the children facing you, even if they have to turn their chairs around. Make sure they have sufficient room to sit comfortably.

Think about where you should stand. If you are in front of a window, it may be difficult for the children to focus their attention on you. Can you make the accoustics better by moving yourself, the children or by re-positioning a display? Is the room too hot? Is there sufficient ventilation?

Plan your time. Have you allowed too much or too little? If you are reading a book in instalments you will need to decide where the best place to stop is. You will also need to allow some time for discussion and reflection.

Techniques

Practise breath control and clarity of articulation, breathing from the diaphragm rather than the chest. Don't add volume to make yourself heard; projection is more a matter of energy from the diaphragm. Use a tape recorder to assess your performance and refine your skills.

Reading aloud is not just a matter of physical technique however. With practice your confidence will grow and you will be able to experiment with your own voice and to use your surroundings and props to help create an atmosphere.

There are several things you can do to enhance your presentation. First of all it may help to play some music to set the appropriate atmosphere. Depending on the story you might like to alter the sitting arrangements. Perhaps you could have the children sitting on the floor in a group to make the sharing of the text a more intimate matter, or darken the room, or read outside on the grass under a tree on a summer afternoon.

Normal conversation speech is too fast for reading aloud. Your voice will carry better and clearer if you slow down.

Hold the book at eye level, slightly to one side, so that your voice is directed neither downwards nor into the book. Children with aural difficulties will then be

Using props helps to create an atmosphere.

able to hear you much better and will also be able to watch your lips if they are in the habit of partially lip-reading.

Where a character shouts, shout; where a character whispers, whisper, directing your voice at the centre of the opposite wall.

Try to apply distinctions between the characters even if you can't do accents. You can make the characters easily discernible by making them a little bit larger than life.

Use physical gestures. If the text says 'he raised his hand as though to hit out',

raise your arm as you're saying it and make direct eye contact with one of the listeners. It all adds drama.

Frequent eye contact will link the children to you. It will help you to gauge their response and also keep control. Try not to break into the story to remonstrate with a disruptive individual. Carry on with the reading whilst moving her to a safe position. This will let everybody know that it's the story that's important and it will not be disturbed for anyone.

Selecting books

Objectives

In order to produce 'real readers' ie children who will grow up to read because they want to, primary schools must promote reading as an activity that is worthwhile for its own sake, by widening the children's reading horizons.

Level of development

At all stages.

Classroom organisation

Provide all kinds of books, at all levels and at all times. As only you know whether you want to read a particular book at a particular moment, or whether you would rather sit down with a magazine (or *War and Peace!*), children are the same. Only a child knows what he wants to read at a particular time. Only he knows what's happening in his world to affect his needs and emotions.

The best way to know what a child

needs to read is to listen to what the children say; when they huddle together in a corner talking about books they get each other reading, by personal recommendation. Listen to parents – they're the ones who know what older brothers and sisters have enjoyed reading or what the child has asked gran to buy him for Christmas.

Keep in touch with the school bookshop – this will tell you what the most popular sales are; what the children are reading avidly.

Providing guidance

Guide the child, without imposing your own idea of what is 'good' (who says 'great literature' is 'great'?) or worthwhile. Lead a child who reads nothing but fantasy/mystery/school stories into other pastures – but gently.

Children often find it easier to 'get into' a book when they are familiar with the author – give them the pleasure of browsing, enabling them time to develop the kind of haphazard searching that leads to something that suddenly excites them. Be there to encourage, stimulate, discuss and make suggestions. Give them the confidence to 'test the water' and try something new.

The sales of the school bookshop will be able to tell you what the most popular books are

Provide as wide a range as you possibly can, aiming at complete fulfilment for every member of your class.

Follow-up

Encourage the children to read for themselves – widely, voraciously, and indiscriminately – so that they can discover for themselves how to assess and compare what they are reading. From this seemingly haphazard experience they will learn to select. The golden rule always is: guide but do not impose. Remember Samuel Johnson's plea: 'I would let a child first read *any* English book which happens to engage his attention; because you have done a great deal when you have brought him to have entertainment from a book. He'll get better books afterwards.' Ha! I hear you say, Perhaps he won't get *better* books. My answer to that is 'What's better?' Keep them reading at all costs, whilst they are *still* reading there is always hope for widening their horizons. But once they give up, you have lost!

Ability

Children left totally free to choose books, without any guidance whatsoever, can actually develop negative attitudes towards reading. If they consistently pick up books beyond their ability, they will eventually receive the message that reading is something that is too hard. On the other hand, if a child was always to select books which are 'too easy', he would be establishing the habit of pleasurable reading, but it would be a pity for you not to extend upon his ability. Clearly some indication of 'match' is required.

The Five Finger Test (Johnson, 1973) can be used spontaneously by the child to grade books. Basically, the child opens the book at about the middle, on a page without illustrations, and begins to read. If he comes to a word he cannot read, he places one finger on it. On the next word he doesn't know he places another finger, and so on. If he needs to place all four fingers and thumb of one hand on a page the possibility is that approximately one word in each hundred will be unknown and the book will most likely be too difficult for him.

You can modify this approach to give a difficulty level of about one in three hundred words, by using the five fingers over five pages – if the child can read five

pages without using up five fingers then he should be able to tackle the book with ease.

More fluent readers should be able to pinpoint the comprehension readability of their texts by using the same method without any difficulty.

Talking about books

THOMAS
THE TANK ENGINE

Objectives

To bring about the kind of informal conversation which leads to mutual sharing of reading experiences.

Level of development

Whole range.

Classroom organisation

'Have you read this book?' sessions can be spontaneous and lead to discussion and recommendations which will be of ultimate value to the children. You can help to promote the discussion by posing a few questions, such as, 'Did the book turn out to be what you expected? What particularly

145

caught your attention about it? What do you think you should tell your friends about it? What parts did you like best? What parts didn't you like at all? How did they make you feel? Was there anything you didn't understand? Has anything like this ever happened to you? Would your reactions be the same? Was the story fast? Which character did you like best? What about the place the story happened in? Was it special? Could it have happened anywhere? Did you see the place in your mind? What made you see it? Would you read the story again? Would you read it to someone else?'

Follow-up

Make a display or graffiti board, where the children can pin up their reviews, criticisms, pictures, cartoons, recommendations etc without having to ask you or work in their exercise books.

Look for articles and features on particular authors or books and pin them up for the children to read. Start a 'Have you read this Book?' scrapbook.

Fiction-based project work

Objectives

To develop pleasure in reading, satisfaction in achievement, curiosity, high expectation of own performance at the same time as refining writing, comprehension and presentation skills, and learning to listen, question and discuss books.

Level of development

Junior age children can get a great deal of satisfaction and develop their language skills from work on a fiction-based project.

Classroom organisation

Select an exciting book that everybody is likely to enjoy, and be prepared for it to take over the whole of your language and art and craft work for the next few weeks! Start by reading the book to the class over a period of time to form the basis of the topic. Try to have several copies of the book to hand so that the children can refer to the text when they need to.

Provide large sugar paper booklets and rough notebooks instead of exercise books in which they can work out their ideas and chapters (these should not be 'marked'!)

When they have sorted out their ideas the children can start to make their own books, following the sequence of the story. These should be as attractive as possible; only their very best material from their rough notebooks should be stuck in. They should choose striking colours and make bold illustrations, use gimmicks like pop-up figures (easily made by fixing a concertina-shaped piece of card to the back of a cut-out), monsters lurking behind opening doors, textured stick-ons, etc.

Get the children to refer constantly to the text for detail when doing their illustrations and encourage them to borrow the book for checking their ideas.

Pick out the most startling or emotionally stimulating passages as the story progresses and discuss them fully with the children; through talking about common responses to happenings or emotions the children will enrich their vocabulary and sort out their ideas enough to express them in writing.

A great amount of the work in their rough books will be worthy of inclusion in their 'master' copy but it wouldn't be fair to expect them to re-write everything. Instead, help them to select the passages that will move the story forwards and give balance to the plot.

Follow-up

Display large pictures of the characters in the book around the room to help the children to identify with them. Make plans or trees of friendship groups, family groups; make friezes of settings or high points in the plot. Discuss 'What will happen next?' 'What if . . .' 'Why should . . .' Be prepared to extend discussions beyond the basic story.

Extending the story

Objectives

To get as much from the story as you possibly can – without spoiling it!

Level of development

Whole range.

Classroom organisation

These are just a few basic ideas for extending the book:

Things to discuss

Relationships; character – how a certain character develops from what happens in the plot; themes; emotional responses to situations that arise; parallel situations the children may have experienced; conflicts and how they are dealt with; the protagonist's problems from another perspective.

Things to do

Build models; make pop-up pictures; draw posters; review; recommend; improvise situations; illustrate; create new book jackets; research any topic that arises; back up newly acquired general knowledge; tape-record discussions, reviews and/or improvisations; retell the story from another point of view; prepare a scripted drama and perform/record it; explore similar situations. You will need to provide a variety of art and craft materials, tape recorders, and plenty of space for drama.

Follow-up

Let the children make their own suggestions for extension work. Guide them to follow where their imagination leads them.

Displays

Objectives

To make a focal point of attractive books in order to tempt the children to read them. The whole point is to lead the children into something more than browsing or dabbling. The initial attraction of the books should be such that it motivates them towards absorbed reading.

Level of development

Throughout the school.

Classroom organisation

Remember that displays depend upon visual impact. They must be attractive to the eye. Don't use old, dilapidated, tatty books that will only put children off. Your selection should take into account not only the content of the story, but the visual appeal of the books themselves – the covers, blurbs and captions are important factors in arousing attention and curiosity.

Choose a well-lit space with plenty of

room for people to stand and browse without being an obstruction. Position the display carefully so that whatever surrounds it does not detract from its appeal.

Use different kinds of materials – colours, textures, shapes – for your background. Use cartoons, building blocks, etc under drapes to achieve different levels and try to include something eyecatching in the centre. Plants and artefacts liven up what could otherwise be a dull display.

Book displays need tidying up at least once every day. By their very nature books beg to be picked up and moved around, so regular maintenance is very necessary.

You can display books on themes:

- new books, just arrived, to create special interest.
- Books with a common theme or message – mystery, historical fiction, school stories and current events.

- Books of film, TV and radio adaptations, etc.
- Books concerned with areas of the curriculum such as nature, sport, science etc.

Displays must be changed frequently. As soon as the children begin to treat the display like wallpaper, you know it has outlived its usefulness. Dismantle it and start again!

Follow-up

Surround the display with work done by children – illustrations, book jackets, stories, poems, junk models, reviews, etc.

Make sure that the books on display are actually available for the children to borrow and read – there is hardly any point in creating an interest in something you cannot supply! If resources are a problem don't forget to use your local library.

A book convention

Objectives

To turn your whole classroom into a display and discussion area, with the children as organisers.

Level of development

Juniors, able to cope with 'something different' in the classroom.

Classroom organisation

Choose a date, weeks in advance, so that you have plenty of time for organising the event. Use the books you have in the classroom, books borrowed from the library, and get the children to bring in their own books from home (carefully labelled of course!) Let the children sort the books into different groups and set up the displays. For instance they might choose to display reference books together, annuals, mysteries etc. Each group of children should work out how they will mount their displays using their desks or tables.

Remind them they have to attract visitors to their section and they should have lots of information and background knowledge to talk about and pass on.

Follow-up

If it works well as an 'in-class' activity, extend it by letting the children invite the whole school and/or parents – they can even work out the timetable themselves (a good problem-solving exercise!)

Book reading club

Objectives

To establish a book-centred social activity, encouraging not just avid readers but others who will 'catch' the enthusiasm of their peers.

Level of development

Most junior school children long to 'belong' and love the idea of clubs. Vary the activities as much as you can so that the reluctant or non-reader can feel just as involved as the fluent reader. Keep the 'club' to small group numbers. Ten to twelve at a time is plenty if it is an extra-curricular activity.

Organisation

The focus of the book reading club should be on informal, interesting, exciting and fun activities with books at their centre.

The choice and selection of books you provide is of crucial importance. Try and provide for wide, indiscriminate reading and for a multiplicity of literacy and cultural experience. Include novels, poetry, drama, short stories, biographies, science fiction, and some non-fiction.

Improvisation

'On-the-spot' acting without scripts:
- use an incident from a book as a starting point for a scene or play.
- use the characters from the book but put them into a different situation.
- explore an experience that's similar to one in the book.

Looking at characters

- Set up an 'interview' between a pupil and a 'character' from the book.
- Encourage a pupil to take on a specific role and tell the story from his point of view.
- Put the characters into new situation and discuss how they will react.

Personal response

- Get the children to make statements about their likes and dislikes. Invite questions from the group.
- Write to the author or publisher with a whole group response to the book – this could include writing, illustrating, collage, montage, etc.
- Work in groups of four to tape discussions about a book or an extract from it.

Reading circle

Get children to read and practise extracts from books that give them particular pleasure. Then ask them to read to the group after giving a short introduction explaining their choice. If you introduce this kind of activity on a regular basis, say once a month, it gives the children something to work towards.

Reading diaries

Some children may want to keep a running commentary on a particular book or on all the books they read. This could be private or for sharing, whichever the child decides. Encourage them to express their feelings about what they have read.

Predicting

Divide the book you are reading into instalments – after each instalment discuss what might be an appropriate next instalment. The children should be encouraged to refine and modify their initial perceptions as the story unfolds so that they are led gently into challenging the author and the text and developing evaluative and critical responses.

Make visits

Arrange trips to book fairs, bookshops, libraries, visiting authors, etc.

Shadow puppets is one way of 'interpreting' a book.

Follow-up

In fact, there is very little difference between classroom activities and club activities – the only difference is the atmosphere you create! If you can create a 'club' atmosphere in your classroom, all the better! I have actually 'conned' a whole class into thinking they were acting as a club for a whole year and they thought it was marvellous that in our class we 'didn't do any work'! All it took was a badge (child-designed circle of card on a pin), a newsboard on the cupboard door and a password – all our language work for the year was then club-oriented and assumed a completely new dimension!

A poetry workshop

Objectives

To encourage the children's response to poetry and foster positive attitudes to it.

Level of development

If you run a poetry workshop as an extra-curricular 'club' activity you can draw children from all over the school; if as a class activity much will depend upon you using poems which provide a 'match' for the emotional level of your pupils.

Organisation

Bear in mind always that most poems need to be read aloud more than once for the children to receive the full 'flavour' of them. Enjoy a variety of poems together, encourage the children to introduce poetry they have found and particularly enjoyed.

Allow the children the freedom to respond in a way that particularly suits them.

Help those who want to do dramatised reading in a group to select music, work out movements, etc to set an atmosphere and make a good visual effect.

Some children may want to draw or paint their response – 'putting the pictures in their head' that the poems evokes on to paper or making a collage or frieze.

Encourage some of the children to write their own poems, either in the same style or along the same theme. Others may want to look for more poems which deal with the same theme or central idea and compare them.

Discussions should be positive. Talk about feelings and reactions should be to enhance the pleasure and delight of the poem; there is nothing to be gained by 'analysing' or 'dissecting' poetry at this stage (indeed, some of us would think, at *any* stage!)

It should be standard practice, when all the extension work is finished, to draw the group together for a final reading of the poem. At this point they will probably want to talk about what it meant to them and what they feel they got out of it. Where such discussion becomes a spontaneous part of the exercise the children are well on their way to becoming poetry lovers for life!

Follow-up

Encourage the children to make their own folders or anthologies. Let the 'club' work towards presenting an account of the workshop to the whole school, perhaps as an assembly, but don't let the presentation become their main aim in attending the workshop.

An anthology of poems

Objectives

To introduce the children to a wide range of form, language, rhythm and ideas. To make the experience of poetry (the awareness of language and how it is used) an enjoyable one.

Level of development

This kind of activity can easily begin in the nursery school with children bringing their own favourite rhymes. A sustained effort

153

throughout the school will have given the children access to thousands of poems by the end of the junior school!

Classroom organisation

Collect, and encourage the children to collect, poems that they like for one reason or another. Every day a poem is read aloud by you or one of the children and pinned to the poetry display board.

They can collect poems on a stated theme and work in pairs or groups to present the poems to the class. The children can experiment with pace and intonation, and present their poems with pictures, puppets or even in costume.

You will need to have a large collection of poetry books available. To help you to get started, a list of recommended poetry books is given at end of this chapter (see page 158).

Organising a 'one-off' event

Objectives

To create a 'Hooked on Books' event which will immerse all the children in the school in books for three days with the aim of promoting awareness of, and an interest in, books. A large, memorable event will hopefully, have good repercussions on the children's reading habits.

Level of development

Whole range.

Organisation

Initiate the support of your colleagues and headteacher. Work out goals and aims together so that there is a consistent pattern and a firm foundation. Three days is a good saturation period, it is long enough for those really interested to display all their flair and enthusiasm and short enough for those against the idea not to get bored!

Contact

Contact the Book Trust for Children's Books (address at the end of this chapter), tell them what you are planning and ask what they can offer.

Book publishers are often prepared to let you have back-up material – posters, promotional materials, etc and, given enough warning may be prepared to offer people to talk to the children – authors, editors etc.

Bookshops will often provide dustcovers, mobiles, posters, etc. They also may provide someone to talk to the children.

Contact:

- 'Writers in the Community' (address at the end of this chapter) who will assist you in locating and paying the fees for a visiting author and/or story-teller.
- Local secondary schools for interested teachers or pupils who will organise a group session eg story-reading, drama, etc.
- Local teacher training colleges who may have students or lecturers eager to take

part in some way.

- Local libraries will provide back-up book material and people who will introduce the library to the children. They can bring materials and tout for custom.

Try and run competitions with books for prizes.

If possible organise a teacher-swap day so that everyone gets the chance to work with a different age group on a story-centred activity.

Display books in every conceivable corner of the school – aim to make every space a book face!

Invite parents to see what's happening. Set up a display where they might like to buy-a-book and donate to the school, or a particular class.

Incorporate a school bookshop area. If you don't already run a school bookshop contact Books for Students (address at the end of this chapter). Allow plenty of time for 'browsing'.

TV 'personalities' such as Postman Pat are always popular visitors.

Running a book club or bookshop

Objectives

To encourage reading for enjoyment and establish book ownership as a pleasurable and normal part of daily life.

Level of development

Throughout the school.

Book clubs

The advantage of a book club is that children regularly receive their own news-sheet with a new selection of books, which they can take home and discuss with their parents. The choosing and buying of the books can then become a shared, family activity. There are many book club operators, but the largest is Scholastic, who run *See-Saw*, *Lucky*, *Chip*, and *Scene* clubs, covering the entire range of children in schools and playgroups. The books on these clubs are offered at discount prices to the children, and teachers receive free posters and divided vouchers to buy books from the *Criterion* selection of educational titles, or exchange for children's titles for the library. The range of books covers a good mix of interests and abilities within each of the age groups. There is a Preview Scheme available for those who want to show the books to the children before they buy.

Book shops

Books for Students offers a vast range of stock – over 20,000 titles – and produces additional booklists of 2,500 titles each term. Books are supplied on a sale-or-return basis. You will need to devote considerable time to updating your shop. Discounts start at 15 per cent but you must obtain a book agent's licence first.

The advantage of a bookshop is that children can handle the books and browse. However, if it is to be successful, it needs a lot of enthusiastic input from staff and parents, and security can be a headache. Inevitably the shop will need to function during the lunch hour or after school.

A lively, interesting display area of selected titles is a good idea. Remember to change the display regularly.

Always take time to read through the club news or bookshop lists with the children as their tastes will not always coincide with yours.

Involve parents as much as possible, since their attitude towards books will undoubtedly influence their children.

Enjoy them yourself!

Objectives

If you find yourself bored with children's books, it's probably because you're not choosing from a wide enough spectrum. Take some time to explore the books which are currently being published. It's amazing how difficult it is to keep up with the world of children's books. Old favourites are fine but just because one class of children enjoyed a book doesn't mean every class will. There are so many good books about, it's a pity not to keep yourself up-to-date. Knowledge of the books available will help you to be able to offer a child a book that deals with the exact problem she's experiencing at the moment.

Level of development

Whole range.

Classroom organisation

Try to get as many other staff members as possible interested in reading and sharing children's books.

If each teacher in the school were to read one new children's book a week, make out a synopsis and set of ideas for extending it, by the end of the year you would end up with a whole boxful of synopses and good ideas! You could either let everyone have copies or keep them in a central point in the staffroom, thus ensuring easy access and a steady interchange of ideas. File the cards in an agreed order (eg alphabetical by author). Stating a rough age range on the cards will help you use the box more selectively. Reviews or articles from magazines can be stuck to your cards, making your task easier.

Even if you can't get all your colleagues motivated, if just one member of staff is prepared to join you, you can get the project off to a good start!

Resources

Addresses

Book Trust for Children's Books, Book House, 45 East Hill, London SW18 2QZ

Writers in the Community, West Midlands Arts Association, West 82 Granville Street, Birmingham B1 2LH

Scholastic Book Clubs, Westfield Road, Southam, Leamington Spa, Warwickshire CV33 0JH

Books for Students, Bird Road, Heathcote, Warwick CV34 6TB

Signal, Nancy Chambers, The Thimble Press, Lockwood, Station Road, South Woodchester, Stroud, Gloucestershire GL5 5QE

Books

The Humorous Verse of Lewis Carrol Lewis Carroll, Constable and Co

Revolting Rhymes Roald Dahl, Picture Puffin

Collected Rhymes and Verses Walter de la Mare, Faber

Old Possum's Book of Practical Cats T S Eliot, Faber

The Complete Nonsense of Edward Lear Edward Lear (ed Holbrook Jackson), Faber

A Book of Bosh Edward Lear (chosen by Brian Alderson), Puffin

You Tell Me Roger McGough and Michael Rosen, Kestrel

Silly Verse for Kids Spike Milligan, Puffin

Complete Poems for Children James Reeves, Heinemann

Mind Your Own Business Michael Rosen, Deutsch

Wouldn't You Like to Know? Michael Rosen, Deutsch

Quick, let's get out of here Michael Rosen, Deutsch

Rabbiting On Kit Wright, Fontana Lions

Hot Dog and Other Poems Kit Wright, Puffin

The Puffin Book of Magic Verse Charles Causley (Ed), Puffin

The Puffin Book of Salt Sea Verse Charles Causley (Ed), Puffin

A First Poetry Book John L Foster (Ed), Oxford University Press

A Second Poetry Book John L Foster (Ed), Oxford University Press

A Third Poetry Book John L Foster (Ed), Oxford University Press

I'll Tell You a Tale Ian Serraillier (Ed), Kestrel

Multicultural approaches to reading

Multicultural approaches to reading

INTRODUCTION

Winsome McKay attended Didsbury Teacher Training College in Manchester. She started teaching at the secondary level but switched to junior school teaching as she felt she would be able to offer children more at that level. She is currently doing an MEd at the University of Birmingham and is employed by The Multicultural Support Services in Birmingham.

Multicultural approaches to education are often regarded as the 'in thing', a fad or the latest educational bandwagon. Multicultural education is then in the same company as 'language across the curriculum' and modern maths which have, in their time, all been described as such. Multicultural education is concerned that all children, whether black, white or shades in between, are being educated to live fulfilling lives in a multiracial society. Multicultural education encourages teachers to examine classroom practice, their attitudes and the language of both staff and pupils.

As multicultural education encompasses all classroom practice, it is essential to begin looking at the basics within the school curriculum, before building on what is hoped will be a solid foundation. As reading is one of the essential three 'R's' all books used must be examined for any sense of bias.

Bias in books

There are those who believe that children should be allowed free access to all sorts of literature, so that they can learn to make decisions about what is good and what is bad. But is such uninhibited access possible in our schools? Are there such unlimited resources? Teachers have to make choices, and these choices should be more positive than negative. All books are biased in some way. Teachers need to develop an awareness of books in which bias is recognised, and then to deal with it in a positive way. Most teachers will agree that immersing children in reading and in written material is important in order that they may learn and absorb ideas. It must therefore follow that if these materials project racist attitudes and perpetuate racist actions these too will be absorbed. Literature can not only broaden horizons, but can also instil attitudes and emotions which will make it virtually impossible for children to relate to other cultures and attitudes different to their own.

Providing opportunities

Teachers should be encouraged to provide pupils with opportunities for exploratory talk in order to clarify and broaden their ideas. Where children are learners of English as their second language, speak Creole or a little-favoured dialect, they have often been seen as being deficient in some way and been placed in remedial classes. The fact that this child may be multilingual

is totally ignored. In a multicultural society therefore, the issue of language and educating for a place in society are inseparable.

Creating a positive environment

There is yet much work which has to be done on all linguistic factors within the classroom. The efforts of the teacher must be directed towards creating a varied and secure language environment in the classroom. Positive values must be placed on the home and community languages of all speakers. Classrooms therefore must become language environments where all pupils, regardless of culture, race or group can learn together. They also must be places where the full range of languages and dialects can be used.

There are now many books available which have a positive bias.

Teaching reading to children learning English as a second language

Objectives

There is a tendency to begin teaching reading to children learning English as their second language too soon, to proceed too quickly, and then wonder why they suddenly come to a full stop. Reading must begin with understanding. Children learning English as a second language face problems which do not arise for children for whom English is the mother tongue.

First, they will be unfamiliar with the sounds occurring in the English language. This makes the phonetic approach to the teaching of reading particularly difficult. English is not a phonetic language, like Welsh or Italian. Take for example, the words 'on' and 'one', or 'great' and 'threat', where the same letter strings are used to produce different sounds. Readers which are constructed on phonetic lines are often absurd and meaningless, eg, 'The pig in a wig did a jig.'

All children, but particularly those trying to come to grips with a new language, will find such sentences confusing.

Second, an unfamiliarity with the syntactical structures of English makes guessing difficult. The anticipation of what has not been seen is vital in reading. Take an imaginary verb, 'to brap', and the noun 'grig'. Without knowing the actual meanings, the correct syntactical structures can be anticipated eg

This is a grig.

These are gr . . .

This grig can brap

Yesterday he b . . . d.

Third, there is a vast amount of vocabulary which children learning English as a second language will not understand, although they may appear to cope very well with English on a day-to-day basis. Teachers need to keep a constant check that these children have a correct understanding of vocabulary.

Finally, because these children may have had different experiences to those which are expected in early learning they may not have the relevant concept information. Because of this, it is important that reading should follow and not be introduced simultaneously with the teaching of the spoken word. When reading is introduced, pupils should only be required to read language they know. Even children who are already literate in their mother tongue may have difficulty transferring to English.

Level of development

Children learning English as a second language can be of any age. Care needs to be taken with older children that they don't feel they are doing 'baby stuff'. Try to find material suitable to each child's age.

Classroom organisation

If possible work with children on an individual or small group basis so that you will be able to give plenty of reinforcement.

Matching games will reinforce basic pre-reading skills and help to develop vocabulary.

Pre-reading skills

Certain pre-reading skills are needed by children of English as a second language prior to their beginning formal reading instruction. Activities such as picture matching, dominoes and lotto etc can be used to help develop the understanding of the concepts of same versus different. By talking with the children and asking questions, eg 'This is a dog. Do you have a dog also? Is yours the same?' you will give them experience with forming questions.

Simple story sequences are important for teaching the concept of time, and the correct use of tenses. These can be bought commercially or be home made. If you don't feel very artistic you can cut pictures from magazines and paste them onto pieces of card. Four or five cards per story is plenty to start with. Choose topics which will be of interest to the children.

Talk to the children as they work to help them develop their vocabulary. Don't forget to stress basic left to right orientation.

Making personal books

The whole sentence approach is better than the 'Look and Say' approach for the initial teaching of reading, because it fulfils the two basic principles underlying the teaching of reading: *interest and meaning.*

Reading should be based upon oral structures already acquired. Start by writing down the children's speech, eg
I am Ranjit.
I like apples.
I live in a flat.

Older children enjoy making games and writing stories for younger children.

Let the children make personal books. Either you or the child should write down the sentences in a small notebook with 6 to 8 pages. Let them design the cover and draw illustrations. You should encourage the children to read their stories aloud to you or to each other. As with any school-made books you should treat them with the same respect as any other book.

Other ideas for stories to make are:
What's this?
It's a . . .
No/Yes, it's a . . .

I am . . .
What are you?

Use a variety of tenses including the present continuous, eg What's he doing? He's skipping.

The children's oral language can also be reinforced with commercially produced books. Try using such books as: Methuen; *Do You Know* Word Books, Instant Readers. Longmans; *I Can Skip/Jump* series, *This is the Way I Go.* Rideout; *I can see – a bus/a ship.* Alexander; *I am long/tall/round* etc.

Matching cards

Picture/sentence matching cards based on structures known orally can also be used. These can be made easily from pictures taken from magazines. Once the children are used to the activity they may like to make their own cards. Let them choose pictures and write appropriate sentences. They can then test each other.

Games

Make flashcards with simple instructions, eg 'Stand up', 'Come here', 'Go to the window' etc. These can then be used to play 'Simon says'.

Other large flashcards can be made to be placed in the appropriate place in the classroom by the child eg 'These are our books', 'This is a door', etc. When all the flashcards have been distributed around the room they could be left there until the next time the game is played.

Children will enjoy playing 'glory bag games'. Make or buy a small bag. Hold up a card and ask the child to point to an object, or ask the child to find an object in the glory bag after reading the card.

The child should also be taught to recognise individual words. Use matching picture and word cards to play games such as snap and lotto. Use word cards to label different items around the room.

After the child is familiar with the sounds of the English language then the initial sounds can be taught. A useful way to start is with a glory bag. Prepare a large card with boxes for each letter of the alphabet. Ask the child to take an object from the bag and place it by the correct letter.

The game of bingo can also be adapted to teach initial sounds. Make cards with letters written in different colours and sizes. You can then call out 'yellow b' or 'red c'. Other games and activities for encouraging letter/sound links can be found in the chapter on 'Word attack skills' (see page 99).

Once the children are familiar with the letters sounds you can start to teach the name and sound. Blends, digraphs and three-letter words can follow in the same way. Make bingo cards using common words. At the end of the game let the children try to make up sentences using their words. You may have to provide them with extra link words.

Enhancing reading skills

Teachers must build up the child's expectation that reading is a meaningful process. In order to do this the material used for reading should focus on language which the child already knows orally.

Most reading books are designed for English speaking children. Therefore they do not cater for these children. Carefully examine the linguistic content of each book to see if it links up with the language of the child. You may find it necessary to adapt it or to base the oral language being taught to the child around the books used.

Points to consider when choosing a reader:

- The language of the book should relate to the oral language of the child.
- There should be plenty of *repetition* of the items of language introduced.
- Language items should be presented in situations appropriate to pupils' age and interests.
- New words should be introduced gradually.
- Pictures should relate to the text.
- Print should be large, clear and appropriate to the script used by the teacher in pre-reading material.
- The text and pictures should not identify with any one social class.
- The stereotypical family should be avoided, eg mother, father, son and daughter.
- The language should be natural, eg 'Daddy, come see the puppy', rather than 'Father, come and see the baby dog'.

Using a variety of activities will help to enhance reading skills.

Follow-up

The Bullock report emphasised that often for children studying English as a second language, the second stage of reading ends too soon. Part of the problem lies with the structure of particular extension readers. Children may understand the individual words, but not the structures in which they are used, eg 'In came the King, with the Queen on his arm.' Where was the Queen? The use of 'on his arm' is idiomatic and needs to be taught or modified. Jessie Reid in 1972, found that even children whose first language was English had difficulty with such structures.

The cloze procedure (see page 93) can be used to assess the readability of texts. Choose a particular item of speech, eg pronoun, verb or preposition to be left out of texts to check understanding.

Picture cards can easily be made using old magazine photographs.

Mother tongue maintenance

Objectives

When the issue of mother tongue maintenance arises in school, the predominant response is often, 'They live here now so they should learn English.' The Bullock report emphasised that no child should have to cast off the culture of home as he crosses the school threshold. It is important that children are not cut off from the language(s) of their own communities because they are learning, or speaking English at school. Children who are encouraged to maintain and develop their first language, are more likely to succeed in the acquisition of the second language and in the formal skills of reading and writing than those for whom the first language was suppressed.

Level of development

Appropriate throughout the primary age range.

Classroom organisation

Many teachers look at the many different languages being spoken in their classrooms and wonder *where to begin.*

The first stage is to find out what languages the children speak and/or read. In some inner city schools you may find many different languages in one classroom. As you are not likely to be able to speak Bengali, Italian, Chinese etc fluently, you will need to find people who can help you. Ask the child's parents and other relatives. Many of them will be willing to come into

school to tell stories or give help with translation if asked. Have you a non-teaching help in your school who is bi- or multi-lingual? She could help in the preparation of material. You must also not forget older children in the school.

You will then need to find suitable reading material in the mother tongue. Several publishers produce dual language storybooks and textbooks including Luzac, Bodley Head, and Mantra. Some books such as the Terraced House series have available stick on translations. Even the *Spot* books published by Heinemann are available in Bengali and Chinese.

The main problem in using these books is that unless there is someone proficient in the language who is able to assess the text, it is impossible to gauge the standard of the language.

In addition to commercial books older children and parents can write stories, and make books for younger children. These can be made into class books. Encourage them to include stories and anecdotes from their home life. Photographs will help the books 'come to life'.

Non-teaching assistants can be asked to read stories in the children's mother tongue.

Tape the stories

To give the children more practice reading and listening to their mother tongue ask parents, older brothers and sisters, non-teaching helpers, and other members of the community to read the books (both bought and school made) onto tape for use in the classroom. A listening area can then be set up. Code the tapes in the various languages using colours or symbols. The children can then follow the written story with the aid of the tape. Some authorities have professional translation units which can be called upon to help in schools.

If your school has language masters and a synchrofax machine these can be used for work in any language. Cut an appropriately sized piece of paper to fit over a card not being used, making sure not to cover the recording tape. Fasten it with a paper clip. Re-record the word to be used.

Encourage children to share their own language with the rest of the class. A collection of nursery rhymes, songs, chants, skipping games, jokes etc in different languages is a good idea. These can be displayed on the wall and added to as children bring in more examples. Notices in and around the classroom eg 'Don't forget to bring your PE clothes on Tuesday and Thursday' or 'Be considerate to others' should be written in many languages.

It must not be forgotten that West Indian Creole, and other English dialects are also languages which children bring to school. They too must be supported.

It is not sufficient to pay lip service to a child's first language, while in practice reinforcing the alleged supremacy of the English language. Children are sensitive. They will accept that a teacher is unable to speak their language, but with encouragement will aid the teacher with some of the aforementioned strategies.

Multicultural education

Objectives

Education needs to include the knowledge and understanding of different cultures to help people develop positive images of each other, so that no one is at a disadvantage because of their cultural heritage. Developing a special curriculum area called 'multicultural education' is not the solution.

The entire school curriculum should reflect society's diverse cultures and beliefs. All schools, even those which have very few or no ethnic minority children, should make their children aware of the society in which they have to live.

Teachers need a knowledge of the interdependence of people, and a knowledge of the needs of their pupils. The way in which these needs and inter-dependencies are expressed in different customs, cultures and behaviour patterns is important. Children should be encouraged to note cultural differences and to give rational explanations for them, rather than to make value judgements or to ignore the validity of other cultures.

The teacher must be conscious of differences. The worst thing that could happen to a child, would be for the teacher to be culturally blind, and to treat that child the same as everyone else.

Level of development

Throughout the school.

Classroom organisation

The materials used in the curriculum must be looked at with regards to the needs, wishes and situation of the pupils. The children themselves are an excellent resource. Each child should be helped to draw from their relevant experiences. Work

Multicultural education is for all children, regardless of their background.

can be produced in differing languages with an English translation. Books published in other languages can be used for topic work.

Fables and folklore from around the world provide an excellent starting point for any work on cultural variations. Whatever the country of origin, the same personal qualities, eg honesty, perseverance, courage and consideration occur. Comparisons can also be made between religions. These insights can aid the development of basic knowledge and skills in education contributing towards a full adult life.

Examining books

Books are among the most effective tools for perpetuating the values and legitimising the attitudes of society. If that society is portrayed as white, middle class, with boys doing all the interesting things whilst girls are consigned to the supporting role, is this a true portrayal of the society in which most children live? What about those who come from one parent families, extended families, in care, adopted or fostered. Both children and adults tend to believe the 'evidence' of their eyes. It is therefore important to look at our books and see the messages and values which they are promulgating. Materials used in our classrooms will be assumed to have our approval and that of 'authority'.

Selecting books

Several points need to be taken into consideration when selecting books for use in the classroom:

- Does the book include people from minority groups, and if so, are they token gestures ie one Black, one Indian and one Chinese. Can children from the group depicted identify positively with the characters and can other children learn from them? Do the illustrations show a full range of facial features? *Babylon* by Jil Paton Walsh, published by Deutsch, is an excellent example of a book in which good images are reflected.
- Are the characters stereotyped? Is the mother always at home cooking, knitting and happy or does she go to work, drive a car, get tired etc. Are all the homes standard detached? Stereotyping is an

invidious reinforcer of prejudice.

- Are characters from the ethnic minorities portrayed as decision making and self respecting as eg Clipper in *Save our School* by Gillian Cross? Do books depict ethnic minority adults in positions of authority, eg *Mr Kofi is a Doctor* by Richard Devenish, or as earning parents as in *The Julian Stories* by Ann Cameron, or the *Jafta* series by Hugh Lewin?
- Are historical facts accurate, backgrounds fairly depicted and carefully researched?
- Is the language acceptable, or is it derogatory? For example are blacks called 'slaves' or 'savages' and whites 'people' and 'discoverers'.

Finding books

There are many booklists available specifically dealing with education for a multicultural society. A selection of these have been listed in the Resources list, page 173.

Follow-up

Most multicultural education consists of the token 'three S's' – saris, samosas, and steel bands. After that the child is taught as a middle class English child, regardless of class, colour, creed or mother tongue. The teacher has to be honest enough to develop methods of exploration and understanding of the attitudes to and respect for the identity of others. The teacher also needs to be sensitive enough to start from where the children are, evaluating their needs with an open and professional mind.

At times it will be necessary to present biased, sexist or racist material to children in order to make them aware of other points of view. In short, the teacher has to value the child enough to want her to develop a positive self attitude, in order for her to progress as well as she is able. A child's language is not an appendage. It is a part of the child – it is the child. Take it away and you deny the child her personality and capacity for positive development.

Reading a story in one language and recording it in another is more difficult than it looks.

Resources

The Books for Keeps Guide to Children's Books for a Multicultural Society 8–12 Compiled by Judith Elkin and Pat Triggs

Books for Students Cassette Catalogue Bird Road, Heathcote, Warwick CV34 6TB

Education in a Multicultural Society – A selection bibliography Rachael Evans, Kiln Cottage, Culham, Abingdon, Oxon OX14 4NE

Testing and keeping records

INTRODUCTION

Elaine Goddard-Tame has had many years of experience teaching in primary schools both in this country and in the Bahamas. In 1985 she took her M Ed from Worcester College of Higher Education on the evaluation of home-schools links scheme, approaches to teaching reading and methods of assessing reading. She is now deputy head at Claires C.E. Primary School in Worcester.

Most teachers assess their children's reading continually, and have a fairly good idea of their progress and where they stand in relation to others in the class. However it is sometimes important to carry out a planned and systematic assessment (ie a test) and record the information in a methodical way. It isn't really sufficient to compile a list of pages, books or levels of the reading scheme a child has read, even when it is supplemented with an 'objective' measure of ability or attainment – such as a reading age. Such a record really tells us little about the child's reading.

Changing times

There are three main reasons why teachers need to think again about testing reading and record keeping.

Firstly, more schools are using 'real' books now in order to teach reading – or at least it is less likely that children will be 'on' a certain book of the reading scheme. This means that there is no 'tag' to attach to a child to describe reading ability to parents and others (eg 'She's on Level 3, Book 2').

There is no obvious way to evaluate progress (eg 'She's on Book 6 now and was only on Book 1 at the beginning of the term, so she must be making progress'). There is also nothing to prescribe what teachers should teach next (eg 'She's finished Book 5, so will need to move on to Book 6). When teachers, parents and children are no longer using the in-built structure of a reading scheme for assessment purposes, other methods have to be devised.

Secondly, the concept of what reading is all about is expanding. Reading no longer means simply the ability to decode words – but also the accomplishment of a whole host of skills and processes, together with a set of attitudes and concepts about print. As reading is seen to be a more complex affair, there is a need to widen the concept of testing reading.

Thirdly, teachers are increasingly being asked to prove that they are actually earning their money, by bringing about children's learning. Various government reports have criticised record keeping systems in schools. It is better that children's performance is assessed and recorded from within, rather than from without!

What sorts of tests are there?

Although the word 'test' may send a shudder through many spines, they can be thought of not just as the formalised, published tests, which are associated with time limits and rightness or wrongness, but also as more informal tests, carried out in a less rigorous manner. These may be published, but can also include tests which teachers can make themselves. Teacher-made tests are rather like carefully structured programmes of evaluation, based on reflective and sound classroom practice. Often they are more appropriate than the formal test and they also cost much less money.

Two types of test

Choosing the right test depends on the reasons for assessment. Tests can be thought of as norm-referenced or content-referenced (although some tests could come into both categories). Briefly, norm-referenced tests set out to compare one child's reading ability against others, whilst content-referenced tests assess how an individual child reads.

Norm-referenced tests

Norm-referenced tests are designed to produce a 'norm' against which other children can be compared. They are constructed in order to differentiate between children.

The test constructors make the assumption that reading ability and attainment is like other psychological and physical attributes – and in fact any other phenomena – all of which are 'normally' distributed throughout the population at large. It is, for instance, assumed that most people will be about average height with fewer people shorter and fewer people taller. If everybody's height was measured, it is assumed the results would follow a symmetrical curve.

Teacher made tests are often more appropriate than formal tests.

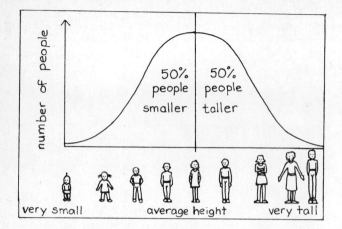

Norm-referenced tests are based on the assumption that reading is the same with 50 per cent of people having reading ability which is lower than average (or the mean) and 50 per cent who have reading above average (with numbers decreasing the further you get from the mid-point).

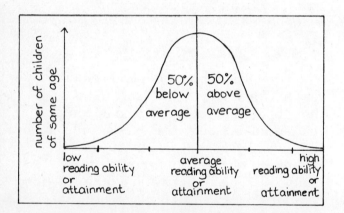

From this normal curve we can determine the percentage of children likely to fall above or below a certain score.

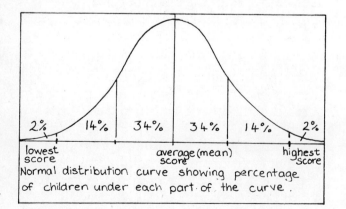

Normal distribution curve showing percentage of children under each part of the curve.

So how does the test constructor establish the average (mean) and normal

distribution in the first place? The test items are written. These are the sentences, passages or words which children 'do' when taking a test, and which are taken as reflecting an aspect or index of reading ability. A large number of children (a sample) then do these items. If items discriminate well between children, ie some children can do them and some can't, and they result in scores lying in a normal distribution curve, they are chosen to be put in the test. If however most children can (or can't) do them, they are thrown out.

Norm-referenced tests are constructed in such a way as to differentiate between children of differing abilities. Fifty per cent of children will score below the average and 50 per cent will score above the average – because the test is designed in such a way as to do this!

Content-referenced tests

Items on a content-referenced test are chosen because they exemplify specific aspects of the process of reading – not because they will produce a normal distribution curve. They are designed to reveal how a particular child reads rather than how she stands in relation to other children. The actual content of the test will depend on how the test constructor thinks children learn to read. For example, if the constructor feels a phonic skills type approach to reading is best the test will reflect this. Criterion-referenced tests tend to stress specific objectives in the teaching of reading. Some reflect a hierarchical model of reading skills acquisition and assess at each level whether the child has mastered those skills. On the other hand however, the emphasis of the test may be different, eg to try to diagnose what the child can't do, rather than what she can. Content-referenced tests have also been created to assess concepts and attitudes.

Teacher-made tests are usually content-referenced. They have the advantage that the teacher can choose items which reflect whatever aspect of reading she wishes to assess. Such tests not only help the teacher to understand the nature of reading better, they also can be tailormade to fit a particular class or child.

Choosing and using a norm-referenced test

Objectives

There are now many norm-referenced tests on the market. They vary in quality and in cost. There are individual tests; tests for group administration; those based on word recognition, sentence completion or cloze procedure; tests based on passages which have to be read and questions answered; tests covering a wide age range and others a narrow age range; those which are expendable and others which can be used time and time again.

The school has to make the decision as to which test to use. This decision is best made in collaboration with all staff, even if all classes are not taking the test. However if there is a person responsible for language development, it is useful if they can get together some samples of tests – either from other schools, language centres or as specimen packs from the publishers (it is rarely possible to obtain inspection copies from publishers).

Norm-referenced tests are intended to be used to compare and discriminate

between children. It is sometimes useful to compare children in your own school with others of the same age. This might be for selection purposes; to give parents an idea of where their child stands in relation to others (they do like to know) or purely for reassurance that standards in school are much the same as anybody else's and your own assessment of reading ability is not completely out of line.

To some extent, the tests can also be used to ascertain the effect of certain teaching procedures or introduction of some new scheme – such as a parental involvement scheme. Few tests however will produce significant differences over any time span less than a year.

Lastly, certain tests, especially those which are to some extent content-referenced tests as well (eg Edinburgh Reading Test and Neale Analysis of Reading Ability), can be used to provide a description of how a child actually reads.

The main objective of these tests is to compare children with the 'norm' so that any statement of reading ability, can only be

179

made in terms of the test and child's performance on that day. To obtain a more detailed description of how a child actually reads – in order to assess progress and plan teaching programmes – content-referenced tests are better, especially those that are teacher-made.

Level of development

There are tests on the market for children as young as six years old, but these more formal types of test are best kept for children who have begun to read fluently. Before this, other types of tests are more appropriate.

In a primary school, children might be tested at seven or eight years for screening purposes and then at ten or eleven at transfer.

Some schools like to test children every year. There is nothing wrong with this, but it is not worth doing the test if the information gained is not put to some purpose. If the sole reason is that it is interesting to compare results over the years or that it provides good practice for the children, then the tests shouldn't be given!

Classroom organisation

The first stage is to decide which test to use. Various factors have to be taken into account.

Age range of children

With the exception of some of the older reading tests, which only assess reading in terms of a 'reading age', most tests are age specific, that is, they take the child's chronological age into account when assessing his performance on a test.

Most tests span one or two years; few span the entire primary age range. Some examples of tests that do are the Group Reading Test (Young 1984) CA (chronological age) range 6.05–12.08 and the Burt Reading Test (Scottish Council for Research into Education 1976) CA range 6.00–12.00. Some tests however do comprise

different stages or levels – such as the Edinburgh Reading Tests (four stages covering age range 7.00–16.00). Care must be taken in comparing the results obtained on different stages however, as there is not always a perfect correlation between them.

Content of the test

The child's reading ability or attainment (whichever the test purports to measure) will be judged on his performance on the test. It is therefore important that the test items mirror as closely as possible, the real act of reading, or at least those aspects which you wish to assess.

Some tests such as Macmillan's Graded Word Reading Test contain a bank of words which the child has to read aloud to the teacher. The child's reading ability can then be assessed in terms of decoding or word recognition.

Tests which contain sentences for the child to read or fill in the missing word, provide the child with extra contextual clues, while tests such as Cloze Reading Test (*Young 1982*) contain passages which take the emphasis away from decoding to a search for meaning.

Tests which measure reading

Tests which measure reading 'comprehension' may include passages to be read, questions to answer, and focus on skills such as finding the main idea, sequencing of ideas, making inferences and rate of reading. A profile may be given, which can be used by the teacher in planning for teaching.

The simpler tests such as word and sentence reading tests are attractive to the busy teacher because they are cheap, easy to administer, and correlate quite highly with other more comprehensive reading tests, but they can provide little information as to how the child reads. Macmillan have tried to get over this problem in their Graded Word Reading Test (1986) by asking the teachers to make an analysis of errors. Word recognition tests however provide a very thin basis upon which to compare children in terms of reading ability.

If word tests are to be used, it would seem more appropriate to base them on words which the child is being taught as part of the reading programme.

It will require a more sophisticated test to measure reading in its wider aspects. Such tests are usually more time consuming and expensive! Cloze procedure type tests are probably the best compromise, especially where the child has to construct her own responses (eg Gap Reading Comprehension Test 1972).(See pages 93 to 94 for futher information on the cloze procedure.)

Tests which measure wider aspects of a child's reading, can also provide extra information for the teacher however – such as Edinburgh Reading Test (*Moray House College of Education* 1982) and may well be worth the extra time and money incurred.

Individual or group test?

Although group tests tend to be more expensive in that they are expendable, their use seems preferable to individual tests. Any time that a teacher has for spending with an individual child is best spent assessing reading informally with the use of content-referenced type procedures (published or teacher-made). Testing would then be carried out to assess an individual's performance rather than to compare him with others (see chapter Hearing children read).

Group tests enable you to give the same test to a large group of children at the same time. Your time spent with individual children can then be used for assessing reading informally.

Time and place of administration

If the test is to be used annually with the same children, then one with parallel forms will be needed. This is a test with alternative test forms but with the same level of difficulty and marking standards. This facility is also useful if children are to be tested in close proximity to each other, such as in the classroom, rather than a hall or dining room.

Purpose of testing

Some tests are designed for specific purposes, for example, the Charteris Reading Test and London Reading Test, are intended for assessing children when they transfer from primary to secondary school.

If tests are carried out to screen for high or low ability, it is necessary to check whether the test can discriminate at these two extremes. Whilst there are a number of tests designed to cater for children of low ability (eg Shortened Edinburgh Test) with a bias in favour of easy questions, it is more difficult to find a test with a high enough ceiling to select the very able children. If a teacher therefore wishes to screen for both levels of ability in one class, she will have to use two different tests catering for different (but overlapping) age ranges.

Qualities of test construction, age and place

The score that a child obtains on the test is a comparison with the performance of a group (sample) of children with whom the test was first tried out. If this happens to be in the Outer Hebrides in 1936, it is likely results of your test will not be very valid! Standards of reading change over the years and vary from place to place. Some tests, such as the Edinburgh Reading Test, have norms (standards which are to be used for comparison) relating to more than one area – in this case Scotland and England. It is best to choose a test which has norms developed in the same country as you will be testing. (Take this into consideration if thinking of using tests from USA or New Zealand if British norms are not given.)

Reliability and validity

Not all tests are 'good' tests statistically.

Reliability means that a test would produce the same results if used over and over again with the same child. Perfect reliability is represented by 1.00, but anything over 0.85 is acceptable. This information and all other regarding the construction of the test should be in the manual. If it isn't, think twice about buying the test!

Validity is the extent to which a test measures what it sets out to measure. The manual should give you some idea as to its validity – although this is usually only as a correlation with other tests.

After choosing the test

Read the manual! It contains all the information you will need for administering the test (or it should do!) Your test results will only be valid if you follow the instructions. So before you administer the test it is wise to read the manual several times over and become familiar with the procedures.

Administering the test

Choose a morning when the children are likely to be alert and motivated (not the last Friday of term!). Explain to them that you want to see how well they can read and there are certain rules which will enable everybody to do their best. Give them general instructions such as hands up if they want anything, the policy on rubbing out and that they must do the test all on their own. Some teachers like to avoid the word 'test', but there seems no harm in using it, so long as it isn't mentioned the night before, so that the children can worry. Have the room prepared beforehand (it is probably better to use a hall if cramped in the classroom) and have a ready supply of pencils and an activity for children who finish first to do (such as a puzzle or colouring). Give the test, following the instructions in the manual (especially those concerning time) and try to maintain a positive, relaxed, pleasant but firm manner with the children.

Interpreting the results

Write names and the children's ages in years and months on the test paper.

Raw scores to standardised scores

When you mark the test you will arrive at a total score called the raw score – that is the number that the child got right on the test. Then look in the manual to find the tables of standardised scores – sometimes called quotients (although they are not strictly a quotient), or standard age scores. Using the

Try to maintain a positive, relaxed but firm manner with the children.

appropriate table, you should then be able to calculate the standardised score using the child's age and raw score. The number will probably be between 70 and 140. This score then tells you how well the child performed in relation to children the same age (the test sample of children).

What is a standardised score?

When the test was first constructed, the mean raw score for a specific age group of children in the original sample was assigned a standard score of 100. All raw scores can then be converted into standardised scores, based on a mean of 100. See the example of a normal curve s.s.

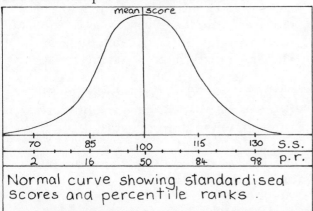

Normal curve showing standardised scores and percentile ranks.

Because it is assumed that the spread of reading ability can be thought to lie in terms of a normal curve – that it is 'normally distributed' – there will be increasingly fewer children who get scores away from the mean. Because the normal curve is symmetrical it is then possible to calculate how many children are likely to get a particular score.

What is a percentile rank?

This type of score is useful in that it gives the percentage of children at a given age group who score at or below a particular score. The manual often gives this information in the form of a percentile rank table. For example:
90 per cent of children will score 130 or below
85 per cent of children will score 115 or below
37 per cent of children will score 95 or below

From this table it can be seen how easily such tests screen children, say in the

bottom or top five per cent and make it possible to compare children.

Is this the child's true score?

No score can ever be considered to be absolutely fixed. The child's score can only be used to define a range of scores within which the true score lies. A statistic called the Standard Error of Measurement defines the actual range of scores where it can be confidently assumed the score will lie.

To be within 95 per cent confidence limits, the range will have to be larger than within 68 per cent confidence limits (the levels of confidence which are usually used in defining the probability of something).

Supposing that in a test with a standard error of ±3 a child scores 109, then it can be said that 2 out of 3 times (68 per cent confidence limits) that his true score will lie within the range of 106 to 112.

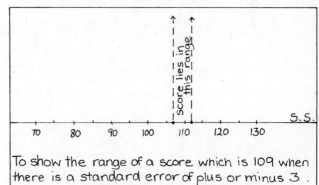

To show the range of a score which is 109 when there is a standard error of plus or minus 3.

The standard error for a test should be given in the manual. It is an important statistic to consider, especially if intending to compare a child's score from year to year in order to measure progress. If a child scores 112 the first year and 106 the next, it does not necessarily mean that she has got worse. It also means that if one child gets 94 and another 100, there is not necessarily any significant difference in their reading ability.

What about reading ages?

Some tests also give tables for the calculation of reading ages. These are entirely different kinds of scores to standardised scores and take no account of a child's age at the time of testing. Instead they provide a 'mental age' for a child who has scored the same raw score as an average child of that age. So if an average six year old (in the tests sample) scored 24 and you had a less able twelve-year-old who scored 24, she would be awarded the reading age of 6.00. The score is misleading in that it is unlikely the reading of the six and twelve-year-old will be qualitatively the same.

Also, reading does not develop in a linear fashion so that it may be more difficult for a child to progress from a reading age of 6.03 to 6.09, than from 9.00 to 10.00. Besides which, the 'average' for the two sexes is different at various ages, yet separate tables are seldom given.

Follow-up

Depending on why the test was administered, different things can be done with the scores.

- If tests are to provide the parents with information, it is suggested that the actual score is not given, unless you are prepared to go into explanations about standard error etc! It is often useful to show them the test and say that their child 'was about average when compared with children of the same age' or was doing well etc.

It's useful to compare the reading in the test, with the level of reading the child is tackling in his reading book.

- If scores are to be recorded on record cards, it is important that the type of test and date of testing is also recorded. It is not unknown for test results to have been compared over the years and suggest amazing progress – when it is just the discrepancies of tests.
- We all like feedback about how we perform. Although some teachers may worry about telling in particular the less able how they performed, it is likely that secrecy can contribute as much to children's dislike of tests as authoritarian measures designed to 'catch them out'. Depending on the test that has been used, it may be profitable to group children according to their results to discuss not only their errors, but how they felt when doing the test.

It is perhaps this information which will give the teacher the greatest insights into children's reading!

Testing early readers

Objectives

By the time children have been in school six months, they can usually manage to read simple texts – some start even before they come to school. However there are occasionally children who cause the teacher to worry, because they appear to have made no progress at all in the first six months. They do not seem able to hear or remember sounds and cannot recognise words, even though they were told them a few minutes previously.

Tests of auditory and visual discrimination are unsatisfactory because even though they may show up weaknesses, they do not provide you with guidance in teaching these children to read. Phonic or word recognition tests aren't much use either because you already know that the child has not mastered such skills. Yet information is needed as to the child's level of reading development, if only to know which type of book to give him.

It is not always appreciated how complex a task learning to read can be for the child. There are many concepts or understandings which need to be developed before the child can be taught decoding skills. The child not only has to learn the conventions of print, eg directionality, but also the links with oral language, eg that a sound is represented by a letter or groups of letters, and the vocabulary which teachers use when teaching reading (eg 'word', 'letter', 'top of page' etc). These concepts develop as a child is read to and with; later reading difficulties are generally associated with a lack of these basic understandings.

Marie Clay's Sand and Stones test can help teachers to test concepts about print. This is an excellent resource along with her two books on reading (see Resources, page 192). You can however make your own test based on books in the classroom. Devising your own test will not only provide an assessment of the child's reading ability, it will also give you a deeper insight into the processes of learning to read.

Level of development

Tests of this nature are best carried out when children have been in school for about half a year and are not showing signs of progress.

Classroom organisation

You will need to have at least ten minutes with the child, preferably in peace away from other children! If it is not possible for somebody else to look after your class, low guidance activities need to be organised to keep other children occupied – perhaps with the guidance of a parent helper. You will need a copy of the record sheet (see page 207) and a book which has a strong storyline, oral language form and simple text.

Sample questions to ask:

1 Will you bring the book over, and put it on the desk in front of me, so we can read a story together from it?
   Check that the child puts book right way in front of you.

2 What do you think this story is going to be about?
   Direct attention to the front cover.

3 There is a picture of a . . . on the front – can you find out what's on the back of the book?
   Check understanding of front/back of book.

4 Now find me the page where I can start reading the story.
   Check that the child finds first page of text.

5 Can you point to where I have to start?
   Check that the child points to print not picture.

6 Which way will I go?
   Check that the child's eye movement and directional sweep of fingers.

7 Where shall I go after that?
   Check left-right orientation and line sequence.

8 As I read the words, you point to them.
   Read slowly but fluently to the end of a page/section.

9 What does that squiggle mean? Do you know what it's called?
   Point to a question mark. Check that the child understands what question is being asked.

10 How are we going to find out . . .?
   Check child understands he has to read on to find out.

11 Can you find another one the same as that?
   Point to a lower case letter, eg 'b'.

12 Can you find a little letter like this?
Point to a capital, eg 'T'.

13 Can you find a big letter like this? (a capital?)
Point to a lower case letter.

14 I wonder if you know what this is for. Do you know what it's called?
Point to exclamation mark.

15 How about this? What is it for?
Point to full stop.
Cover up a word which is repeated frequently in the story, eg 'pig' in the Three Little Pigs.

16 What do you think this word is going to say?
Check use of semantic clues.
Read until you come to a sentence with an '-ing' ending. Cover up the ending.

17 What do you think the end of that word says?
Check use of syntactic clues.
When you come of the end of the story ask:

18 So what happened in the end?
Check appreciation of ending.

19 Show me a word – and another one – and another one.
Check child is not pointing to letters.

20 What's that space for?
Point to spaces between words.
Give child strip of paper to cover top line.

21 Move the paper until you can see one letter . . . now all the letters of the word.
Child should move paper slowly left to right uncovering the first word.

22 Listen to these words – 'bite', 'bark', 'burrow' (choose words from story). They all start with the same sound. Can you say the sound you can hear each time I say them?
Bark . . . Bite . . . Burrow.
Emphasise initial sound.

23 Look at the words as I read them, eg 'Dogs can bark and bite' (point with finger). Show me the letter that makes the 'b' sound. Can you find the 'b' sound anywhere else?
Notice if the child points to a capital B!

24 I'm going to sound a word out that's on this page. You guess what it is. Now another one.
(Visual identification of word can also be tested.)

25 Do you find reading easy? Are you a good reader?

Carrying out the test

This is not a test in the strictest sense and throughout the session you should give the impression that you are sharing a book with the child. Find somewhere to sit down where the child will be able to sit beside you (do not make her stand at your desk!). Use the 'Sample questions to ask' as a framework around which to base your own conversation with the child. Before giving the test you will need to have decided where in the text you will stop to ask each question. You may need to change the order to suit your story. Use the questionnaire in a flexible way, changing wording where necessary. Remember however that ambiguous questions lead to answers that can be interpreted in numerous ways. Try to memorise the questions beforehand. It may take you a while to become experienced in administering the test, before you can expect to 'tap' every one of the concepts listed on the checklist sheet (see page 207).

Recording

Again this is flexible. Try to avoid using ticks and crosses. Brief comments are more useful. Remember the development of concepts is not an all or nothing affair, so you may feel that a child is almost there – but not quite. If you want to use a points system, 2 could be given for each question, although it is possible that you will not want to ask all questions, or manage to extricate responses to each one.

Follow-up

Results on this test can give you ideas for teaching – although it cannot be expected that children will learn new concepts overnight.

Basic ideas about books

Responses to questions such as 2 and 10 will help you to assess whether a child understands that the print in a book is a permanent message – in this case, a story which is told as a sequence of events. Whilst pictures can give a clue as to what is happening in the story, it is the 'black squiggles' which give the precise message. Children at very early stages of reading will tend to focus on the pictures, using them to make up their own story, and in this way 'read' the book! This presents no problem when reading a picture book.

Ask the child what he thinks the story is going to be about from looking at the front cover.

Following print

Questions 1–7 will help you assess whether the child knows which is the front and the back of the book, that we read left to right, and one line after the other. An understanding of punctuation marks will develop later on, but are a good indication of whether the child has reached the stage of understanding strategies used for transposing oral to written language.

The link between oral language and print

Now that more reading books are written in a natural language form, it is easier for children to realise that print is just words they say written down. Questions 16 and 17 can be used to help you assess whether children realise they can use their own knowledge of spoken language to predict words in a text. If they use syntactic cues they will be using their knowledge of grammar. If they are using semantic cues, they will be using the meaning of words.

The relationship between sequences of sounds and words

Questions 19–24 will help you ascertain, not only whether the child can separate sounds in spoken words, use auditory and visual matching and discrimination, but understand that there is a pattern of correspondence between sounds and letters which is constant. Without understanding this, it will be difficult for children to learn 'sounds', especially if taught as separate phonic lessons and the letter is presented with the corresponding sound.

Teaching procedures

Many of these concepts will be developed through writing and reading stories together. The use of a Big Book however can be a useful teaching strategy with a group of children who are having learning difficulties.

Using big books

There are several big books coming on to the market now. Arrange a Big Book on an easel, clipped on with a bulldog clip with children sitting in a semi-circle around you. Read the story to them, modelling the directional movement with your finger. Having talked about the pictures, ask the children questions in relation to the concepts which you are trying to get them to understand. For example:

- Can you put your finger under each word as I read it?
- Who can spot the word . . .?

Big books are useful for informally assessing reading skills.

- Can you put a little finger over one word so that no letters are showing?
- Can you get your thumb in the space between the word . . . and . . .?
- See if you can find one of those dots in another story book (point to a full stop).

Children probably learn most from each other. Afterwards, leave the Big Book in the carpeted book area and encourage children to play 'school' – taking in turns to be teacher, reading the story and asking questions. Eavesdrop and monitor their levels of understanding! (Further ways of using big books are described in the chapter on Shared reading, see pages 40 to 43.)

Keeping a check on fluent readers

Objectives

When children get to the stage of being able to read silently and fluently, it is less likely that you will be hearing them read regularly. It is more difficult therefore to know how individuals are getting on, except by keeping a check on the type and number of books they are reading.

Teachers need a systematic scheme for observing children's reading behaviour, which can be carried out regularly; provides information for further teaching; is a guide to the progress a child is making and is based on evaluation of attitudes to reading as well as assessment of comprehension and decoding skills.

The proposed scheme is based on a checklist of aspects of reading. It involves the use of miscue analysis to assess the strategies a child is using when reading, and questioning to probe literal and inferential comprehension, evaluation and attitudes to reading.

Level of development

The scheme can be adapted to be used with any child who has passed the beginning stages of learning to read. It is suggested that the assessment procedure is carried out at least once a term (preferably twice) and completed record forms are kept in a reading file along with a list of books the child has read. The child could keep this record of books herself – or it could be carried out as part of parental involvement in the reading scheme.

Classroom organisation

Fitting it into the timetable

Put aside one week in the term (maybe the second week) to concentrate on reading. This could be made into a special Book Week or Reading Drive where a large percentage of the timetable revolves around reading activities.

With an average sized class you will need to organise low guidance activities each morning, so that you can give undivided individual attention to six children. This may seem to be rather a lot of time to devote to reading, but remember the advice of the *Extending Beginning Reading* report (Southgate et al) that teachers should hear children read less regularly but more thoroughly – and that even though children

are fluent readers their reading is still developing.

What you need

- A copy of the record form (see page 208).
- A tape recorder if possible
- A passage for the child to read – of which you have a duplicate copy

The passage should be about 400 words long, fairly self contained, and at a level of readability which the child can read, but not without some difficulty. It could be from:

- the child's own book, which you take home the night before to skim and mark an appropriate passage,
- a graded passage taken from Helen Arnold's *Making Sense of It*,
- a selection from a reading scheme book which the child has not read.

You will be more likely to be assessing a child's real reading if you use their own reading book, but the use of set passages (or your own compilation of graded passages) will mean less work.

Your copy could either be a photocopy or a duplicate original, together with an acetate sheet and marker pen. You need to know the approximate readability level of the passages and number of words (these are given, in the manual that goes with *Making Sense of It*). Fill these details in on the record form together with the child's name etc.

An appropriate passage can be chosen from the child's own reading book.

Procedure

- Put the child at ease and explain that she is going to do some reading, but you are not going to help her. She should take no notice of the tape recorder or you writing.
- Ask the child to read the passage aloud and conduct a miscue analysis as described below.
- Ask the child to read the passage again silently to herself and explain you are going to ask her questions about it afterwards (see questions below).

Time how long it takes the child to read the passage silently and calculate speed in words per minute, filling this information in on the record form.

How to carry out a miscue analysis

When a child miscues she deviates from the text. It is not called an error because this suggests a negative mistake. Miscues are not only helpful to the teacher in gleaning information about how a child reads, a child can also miscue when trying to make sense of the text (if a child is given a poorly written text with stilted language, a good reader will miscue many times as she tries to make sense of it!).

As the child reads aloud, mark your copy of the text with the appropriate symbols when the child miscues. (See page 86 for a chart of symbols.) Tape recording the session will provide a back up for information missed (likely if the text is very difficult for the child).

- Look at the substitutions. Has the child used her grammatical knowledge in substituting another word (used syntactic cues?). Has the child used her understanding of the meaning of the text in substituting another word (semantic cues?). Has the child used her phonic knowledge in making the substitution (used graphophonic cues?). Which cueing systems does the child depend on most. Is she trying to extract meaning from the passage or is she just visually decoding?
- Look at reversals. Is there any pattern of reversal of words or letters?
- Look at omissions and insertions. Is there

a pattern in this – do they reflect the child's spoken language?
- Look at repetitions. Why is the child repeating words? Is it when she is thinking about what the next word says or is it a lack of confidence?

Fill in the record form assessing whether the child is making positive or negative miscues. Is the child reading for meaning and which cues should she be encouraged to use? (Fluent readers use all three, whereas children with weak reading strategies tend to concentrate on using graphophonic cues).

Questions to assess comprehension

Once the child has re-read the passage silently, ask these questions with specific reference to the text being used. The first five questions are based on literal comprehension – that is understanding of what is stated explicitly in the text. The remainder are based on inferential comprehension – that is reading between and beyond the lines.

Let the child re-read the passage again silently before asking questions about content.

- Ask the child to recall the answer to a factual question, eg 'What was the name of . . .?' (If the child cannot recall, ask her to look back and find out – that is, recognise rather than recall. Also the opportunity should be taken to see if the child can skim the text.)

- Ask the child what was the main idea of the passage, eg 'If you had to tell somebody what this passage was about in just a few words, what would you say?' (This question may indicate whether the child knows that the title gives the main idea.)
- Ask the child to recall the sequence of events as it happened, eg 'Tell me the main things that happened in the story in the right order.'
- Find out if the child links a stated cause and effect, eg 'Why were you told that . . . happened?'
- Ask the child to recall character traits, eg 'What did it say . . . was like?'
- Ask the child to extract an underlying idea, theme or moral eg '. . . was the main idea of the story, but what is the author really telling you as well?'
- Find out if the child can infer the cause of something which is stated happening in the text, eg 'What do you think made . . . do . . .?'
- Find out if the child can infer the sequence of events, eg 'First of all he . . . What do you think happened between . . . and . . .?'
- Ask the child to infer characterisation, eg 'What would you imagine . . . was like or would have done if . . .?'
- Ask the child to predict an outcome, 'What do you think would happen next if . . .?'

Questions to ask to assess ability to evaluate a text

- Find out if she knows the difference between fact/fiction, myth/legend etc, eg 'What sort of story is this? If we put it in the library . . .'
- Find out if the child can judge the characters, eg 'What do you think about . . . doing . . .?'
- Assess whether the child appreciates the author's use of language, eg 'What do you feel when you read that bit . . . How does the author make you feel like that?'
- Assess whether the child responds emotionally to the passage, eg 'What does the passage make you think about as you read it, or afterwards?'

Discussion about reading

These questions will have to be re-phrased if asked each term!

- Ask the child whether she reads at home, eg 'Have you got many books at home? Are they good ones? Do you like reading them? When do you usually do your reading?'
- Ask about preferences, eg 'If I gave you two pounds to buy something to read, what would you buy?'
- Assess image of self as reader, eg 'Do you think people think you are a good reader? Do you find reading easy or difficult?'
- Assess degree of parental involvement, eg 'Does mum or dad know which book you're on at the moment? Do they ever hear you read or talk to you about your books?'

Follow-up

Once the record form is filled in, it should be used to determine how best the teacher can aid the child's reading developing – for instance this might be to encourage reading for meaning by giving work on group cloze procedure, or working on a particular reversal problem or encouraging children to read with their parents.

The record should also be compared with the previous terms. Hopefully if the child is making progress she will be able to cope with a passage at a higher level of readability, perhaps have increased her speed of reading and be reading between and beyond the lines – not only at the literal level.

For further information on miscue analysis and teaching strategies, Arnold's book provides a useful resource.

Walker and Rye's books contain interesting ideas for teaching extended reading skills to the 'fluent reader'.

This scheme for assessing children's reading may not be as 'objective' as some teachers would like, but it will provide a basis for reflective teaching and research in the classroom and give you a clearer description of how an individual child actually reads.

Resources

Reading Tests and Assessment Techniques
P Pumfrey, Hodder and Stoughton (1985)

Assessment in Schools D Satterley, Basil
Blackwell (1981)

*Reading Tests in the Classroom: an
introduction* D Vincent, NFER – Nelson
(1985)

Measuring Reading Abilities P Pumfrey,
Hodder and Stoughton (1977)

Testing for Teaching F Spooncer, Hodder and
Stoughton (1983)

The Early Detection of Reading Difficulties
(2nd edition) M Clay, Heinemann (1981)

The Patterning of Complex Behaviour M Clay,
Heinemann (1984)

Making Sense of It H Arnold, Hodder and
Stoughton (1984)

Extending Beginning Reading Southgate V et
al, Heinemann Educational Books (1981)

Cloze Procedure and the Teaching of Reading
J Rye, Heinemann Educational Books (1984)

Record sheets for pages 77 and 80

Paired reading record	Name:			
Day	Book chosen	Time spent	With whom?	Comments
Monday				
Tuesday				
Wednesday				
Thursday				
Friday				
Saturday				
Sunday				

Teacher's comment: Signed: Date:

Guided listening record	Name:		
Date	Book read	Pages read	Comments

Teacher's comment: Signed: Date:

Paired reading procedure (see page 80)

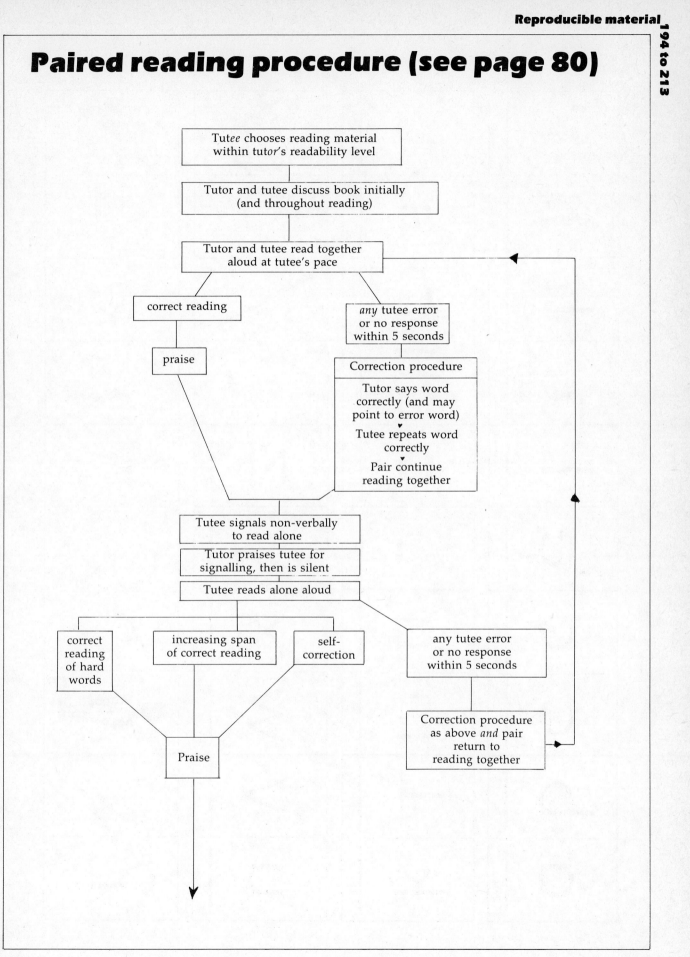

Tutee chooses reading material
within tutor's readability level

Tutor and tutee discuss book initially
(and throughout reading)

Tutor and tutee read together
aloud at tutee's pace

correct reading

praise

any tutee error
or no response
within 5 seconds

Correction procedure

Tutor says word
correctly (and may
point to error word)

Tutee repeats word
correctly

Pair continue
reading together

Tutee signals non-verbally
to read alone

Tutor praises tutee for
signalling, then is silent

Tutee reads alone aloud

correct
reading
of hard
words

increasing span
of correct reading

self-
correction

any tutee error
or no response
within 5 seconds

Correction procedure
as above *and* pair
return to
reading together

Praise

Letter cards (see pages 105 and 106)

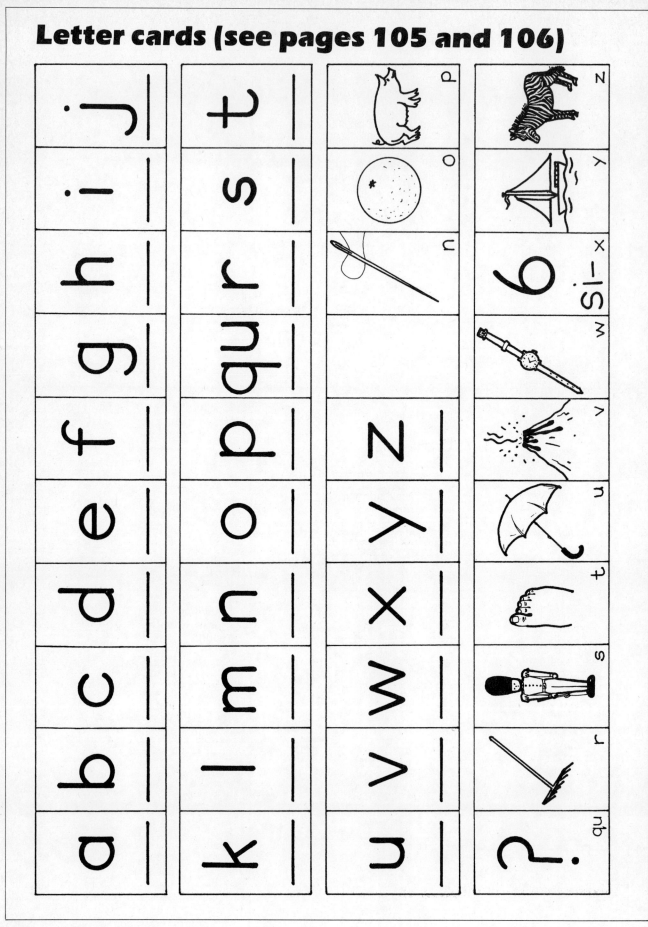

Letter cards (see pages 105 and 106)

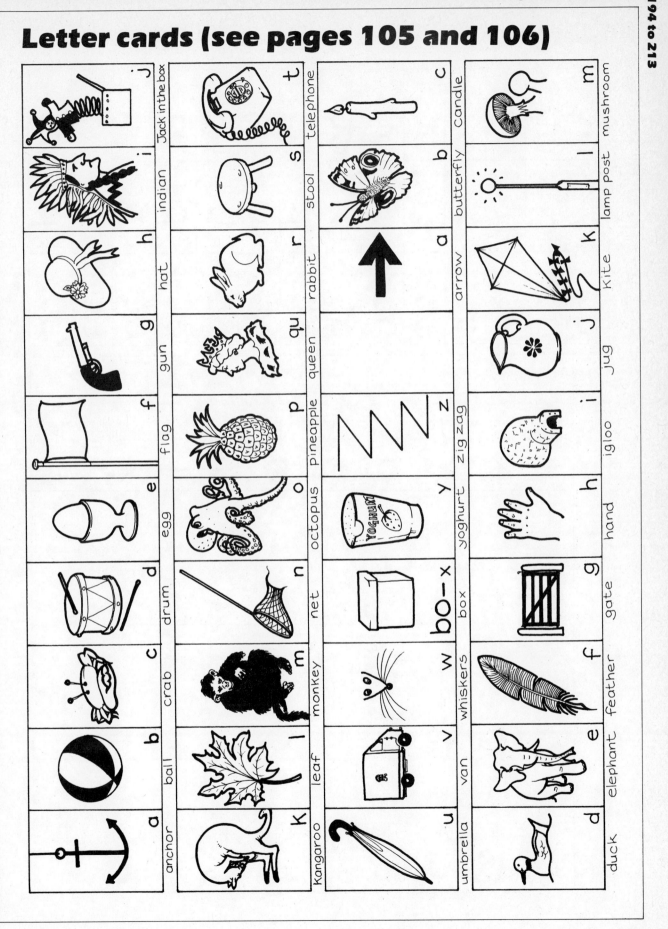

j Jack in the box
i indian
h hat
g gun
f flag
e egg
d drum
c crab
b ball
a anchor

t telephone
s stool
r rabbit
qu queen
p pineapple
o octopus
n net
m monkey
l leaf
k kangaroo

c candle
b butterfly
a arrow
z zig zag
y yoghurt
x box
w whiskers
v van
u umbrella

m mushroom
l lamp post
k kite
j jug
i igloo
h hand
g gate
f feather
e elephant
d duck

Long card game (see page 110)

ot	ot	ot	ot	ot	ot	ot	ug	ug	ug	ug	ug	ug	ug
ip	ip	ip	ip	ip	ip	ip	op	op	op	op	op	op	op
at	at	at	at	at	at	at	et	et	et	et	et	et	et

r	b	f	g	p	s	m	l	t	d

s	d	f	j	m	b	l	n	p	t

n	p	t	r	b	g	h	c	t	m

t	p	c	b	s	h	j	m	r	l

Die board for long card game (see page 111)

⚅	ug
⚃	op
⚁	ip
⚂	ot
⚁	et
⚀	at

Sound blending wheel (see page 111)

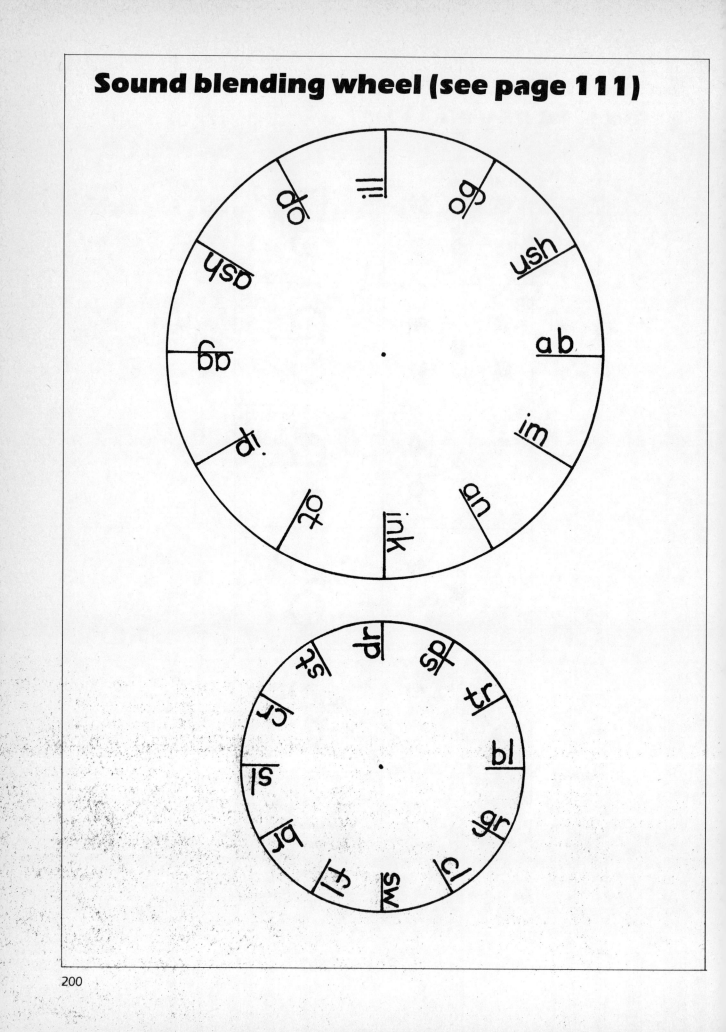

Noughts and crosses (see page 112)

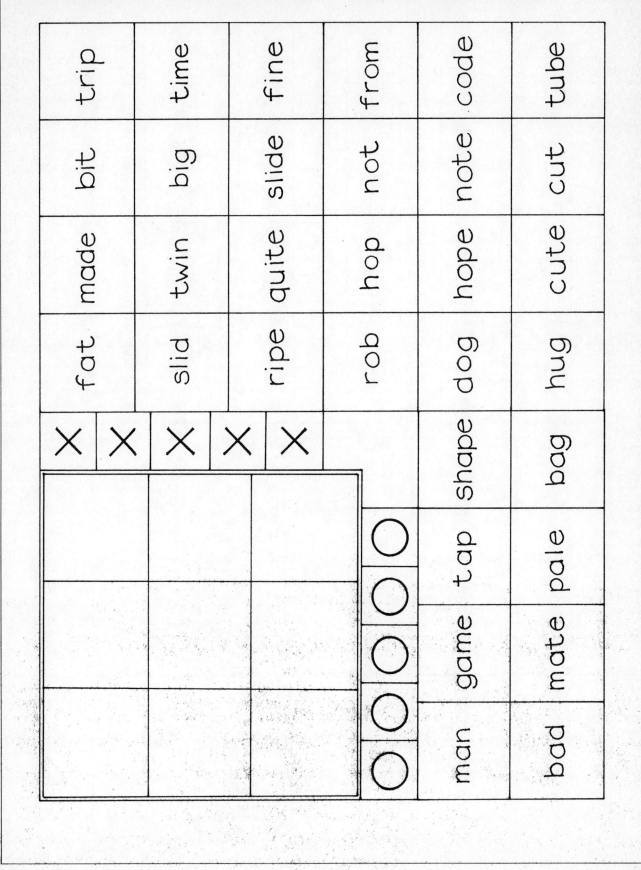

trip	time	fine	from	code	tube
bit	big	slide	not	note	cut
made	twin	quite	hop	hope	cute
fat	slid	ripe	rob	dog	hug
X	X	X	X	X	shape	bag
			○	tap	pale
			○	game	mate
			○	man	bad
			○		
			○		

Lotto (see page 112)

(see page 112)

LOTTO CARD 1

decide	except	centre	necessary
certainly	success	exciting	circus
December	pencil	cycle	conceal

LOTTO CARD 2

city	necessary	circle	central
excited	certain	except	accident
recent	parcel	century	decent

LOTTO CARD 3

circle	accept	decide	centre
certain	citizen	recently	circumstance
mice	innocent	concert	civil

CALLER'S CARDS

accept	accident	central	centre
centre	century	certain	certain
certainly	circle	circle	circumstance
circus	citizen	city	civil
conceal	concert	cycle	December
decent	decide	decide	except
except	exciting	excited	innocent
mice	necessary	necessary	parcel
pencil	recent	recently	success

Switch game (see page 113)

oa soap	oo broom	igh right	oo boot
oa moan	oo food	oo tooth	ee sleep
oa goal	oo loop	oo soon	ee weeds
oa road	oa load	oo room	ai wait

ai strain	ee seem	igh light	oa boat
ai gain	ee tree	igh fight	igh tight
ai tail	ee feel	ee need	igh night
ai rain	ai paid	ee been	igh might

Road sense (see page 114)

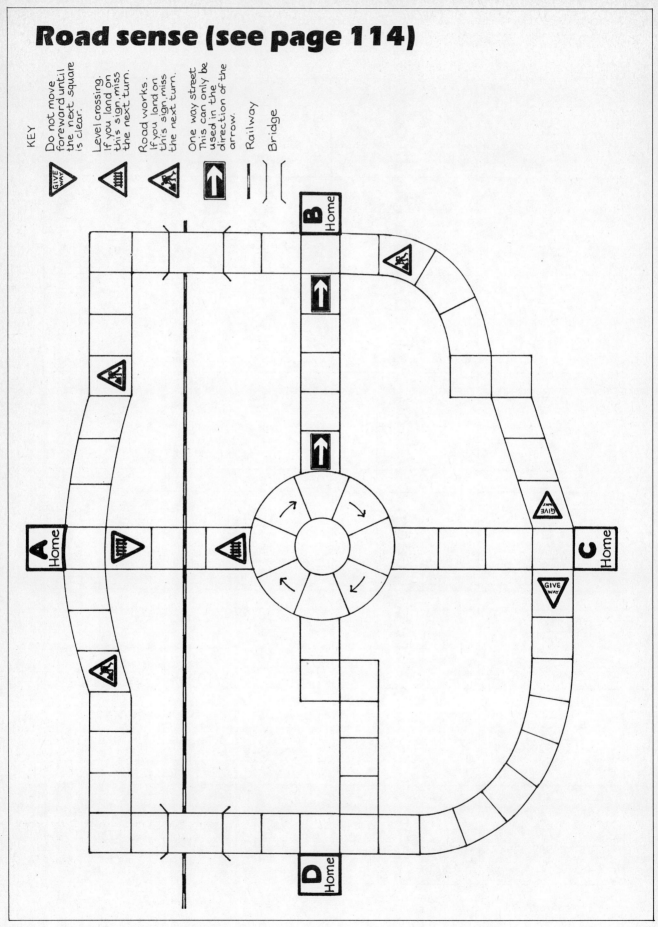

Double sound words for Road sense (see page 114)

saucer	fault	haunted	August	shawl
A lawn	outlaw	straw	yawn	awful
B third	thirsty	skirt	flirt	dirty
C shirt	return	nurse	disturb	curl
D church	burst	purse	learn	early
search	earth	pearl	earn	because

voice	toilet	avoid	poison	joint
awkward	point	coin	convoy	destroy
employ	annoy	enjoy	envoy	ground
county	amount	trousers	account	found
mouse	allow	power	tower	drown
brown	growl	crowd	cause	applause

Syllable sums (see page 115)

ex	ho	chop	jo	ska
ex	ho	sha	re	mi
ex	pre	sha	re	mi
in	pre	ha	run	con
in	pre	ha	run	con
in	chop	jo	ska	con

END syllables   Cut out along the lines and cut off shaded corners.

tend	ning	tent	king	port
tend	ning	tent	fer	port
tend	ner	tent	fer	vent
tend	ner	ker	fer	vent
ting	ted	ker	ped	ping
ting	ted	king	ped	ping

Early reading record (see page 189)

Name: Age: Class: Date:

Book: Readability level:

Page	Concept	Response	Score
	1 Orientation of book 2 Pictures relate to story 3 Front/back of book 4 Left page read before right 5 Start top left of print 6 Read left to right 7 Line sequence 8 Written words represents spoken 9 Function and name of '?' 10 Story is told as sequence of events 11 Letter matching 12 Match lower to upper case 13 Match upper to lower case 14 Function and name of '!' 15 Function and name of '.' 16 Predictability using semantic cues 17 Predictability using syntactic cues 18 End of story 19 Concept of a word 20 Function of a space 21 Concept of a letter 22 Concept of a sound 23 A sound is represented by a letter(s) 24 A word is a blend of sounds 25 Concept of self as reader 26 Other responses		

Reading record form (see page 189)

Name: Age: Class: Date:
Text used:
Readability level: No. words:

Words per minute (silent):
No. of Errors (oral):   %
No. comprehension questions correct: %
Reading level Independent: Instructional: Frustrational:
Eye/lip movement:
Finger pointing:

Silent reading – comprehensive
1 Can recall facts:
2 Can state main idea:
3 Can recall sequence:
4 Can connect cause and effect:
5 Can recall character traits:
6 Can infer main idea not stated eg moral
7 Can infer cause and effect:
8 Can infer sequence:
9 Can infer character traits:
10 Can predict outcomes:

Evaluation
1 Can judge nature of text:
2 Can judge characters:
3 Appreciates author's use of language:
4 Emotional response to content:

Oral reading – Miscues   +   –
1 Substitutions
    Graphophonic:
    Syntactic:
    Semantic:
2 Reversals
3 Omissions/additions
4 Repetition/looses place

Approach to reading
1 Can choose appropriate level:
2 Reads of own accord:
3 Prefers fact/fiction:
4 Self concept:
5 Parental involvement:
6 Any other notes:

Dos and don'ts of reading (see page 77)

Here are a few simple Dos and Don'ts to remember when you are reading with your child.

Do
keep the sessions short – no more than ten minutes.

Do
read as often as you can find the time. Try to read at least three times a week.

Do
make sure the atmosphere is relaxed and happy.

Do
let your child sit very close to you.

Do
give plenty of praise.

Do
read with your child. It is often more fun to read a page together or take turns with each sentence.

Do
give your child plenty of time to read to you.

Do
encourage your child to guess at any words he or she can't read.

Do
tell your child the beginning sounds if he or she can't guess. If this still doesn't help, just tell your child the word straight away, and carry on reading. Don't make an issue of it.

Do
look at and discuss the pictures.

Do
talk to your child about the book.

Do
make sure your child enjoys the time together.

Don't
make reading an unpleasant task.

Don't
have the television on.

Don't
threaten to put your child to bed early or tell the teacher if he or she doesn't do well.

Don't
make your child feel he or she is in competition with anyone else.

Don't
worry about lack of progress.

Don't
be afraid to ask for help and advice, however small the reason might seem.

Note to teachers

The following pages can be made into a small booklet for you to give to parents. It is intended to be used as a supplement to the list of Dos and don'ts on page 209.

The way reading is taught varies greatly from school to school, and even from teacher to teacher. As a result, some of the suggestions or comments made in the following booklet may be different from the way things are done in your school. The ideal booklet would, of course, be one tailor-made for your school and many schools have already written their own. Please feel free to modify the contents of the booklet to suit your school and classroom. We hope you will find it useful whether you use all or just a part of it.

Helping your child to read
A parents' guide

Dear Parents,
Learning to read is one of the most important things children do in primary school. We are often asked by parents how they can help. A frequent comment is that the methods used today are so different from the way that they remember being taught that they don't know where to begin. The purpose of this booklet is to explain how and why reading is taught the way it is taught in this school and how you can help. If you have any queries after reading the booklet, or would like to know more, please do not hesitate to see your child's teacher. She will be very glad to help.

The main philosophy behind the way we teach reading is: Why make it more difficult than it needs to be?

Think of the way other things are learned. Adults

2

learn to drive by driving; children learn to swim by swimming. To begin with they need a lot of support, but it is through actually swimming or driving that they learn. Why not teach reading in the same way? Instead of teaching individual words or sentences taken out of context, why not give children books with good stories which they will want to read? As with any other activity, the children will need help to begin with. They will need someone to read the book with them. Through listening and talking about books your child will learn how to read, and because having someone read good stories with you is fun, they will want to keep on doing it.

Reading is a very demanding activity for young children. There are so many things they need to learn, things adults know and do so instinctively that most of us have forgotten they had to be learned. They need to learn what a letter is and that each letter has a sound. They need to learn what a word is and that a space means the end of one word and the start of the next. They even need to learn to read print from left to right and down the page.

3

With so many things to learn, it is important that children see a purpose to reading. If their only experience with reading is from books that don't have a story and which they don't find terribly interesting, they won't be motivated to read. Some reading scheme books have a very limited vocabulary and no story line. Their emphasis is on word recognition, rather than on reading for meaning. It is very difficult for children to learn to read from such books. This is why we don't use them in this school. Instead we offer children books with 'good stories'.

Our school has a large range of books for children. Some tell stories, others give information. Some are based on everyday experiences, others are traditional tales. Some are easy to read, others are more difficult. Some have illustrations, others don't. All the books have been chosen because we think children will enjoy them.

4

We allow children to choose which book they would like to read. Giving them the choice gives them an extra incentive to learn to read. They do not need to read the books in any particular order or read one set of books before moving on to another set. The teacher will, of course, sometimes make suggestions. For example, she might say, 'Have you tried reading this book. It is by the same author as the one you read last week' or 'I know you like reading stories about horses. Have you tried reading this one?' In this way she can help to guide the child's progress.

In school the teacher will read books to and with your child. As she reads with him she will point out different words and letters; he will encourage him to join in with the story or to tell it in his own words. At first he won't be word perfect. This does not matter as the teacher will be there to guide him.

5

Your child will also be given the opportunity to write his own books. Initially he will need the teacher's help to write the words down. Later he will be able to write on his own. These will be stories about things he knows and cares about: himself, his family and everyday happenings. Because he has written them and they are about things which he cares about, he will enjoy reading them to you, to his teacher and to other children. Writing and reading one's own books is an important part of the whole process of learning to read because it helps children to understand that reading has a real purpose.

How is progress recorded?
Throughout the day the class teacher will be observing the children. Often it is what children do on their own that reveals most about their

level of understanding. The teacher has charts on
which to record what books each child has read
and their knowledge of reading skills. With
these records she can then plan activities which
will help them learn the skills they are lacking.

6

How can you help?
Your child will bring home a book in a book bag.
This will be a book which he has chosen. We do
not expect you to 'teach' your child to read. All
you need to do is read to your child. Your child's
teacher can give you a simple list of dos and
don'ts to help you. Look at the pictures together,
talk about the book as you read. When your
child gets better at reading he will probably
want to join in. Don't force him to though. It is
better for it to come naturally than for him to feel
as if you are testing him. Even when he can read,
there may be some days he might just feel like

listening to the story rather than reading
himself. The most important thing is for both of
you to enjoy it.

7

Children like to own their own books. If you
would like advice on deciding which books to
buy we would be happy to help. A ticket to the
local library is also a great asset.

Headteacher

Index